T0316293

Thomas O'Loughlin is Professor of Historical Theology in the University of Nottingham. His research explores how our understanding of Christian belief can be enriched by seeing how individual expressions of that faith, such as the *Didache*, can be located within the dynamic life of the communities that produced them. 'Tradition' is not, therefore, a weight from the past that pulls a community backwards, but rather is the life of that community, constantly seeking to reinterpret its inheritance in the light of its current experience and hopes. The historical theologian's task is, consequently, that of uncovering how a community inherited, lived, shaped and handed on its vision. O'Loughlin has pursued this study in numerous books and articles over the past 20 years, covering topics relating to the early Church and the early Middle Ages; his passion is training graduate students in this often neglected field of research. He is the editor of the series *Studia Traditionis Theologiae* (Brepols), which is dedicated to the study of theology through the lens of tradition.

THE *DIDACHE*

A window on the earliest Christians

THOMAS O'LOUGHLIN

SPCK

Ｂ
BakerAcademic
a division of Baker Publishing Group
Grand Rapids, Michigan

First published in Great Britain in 2010

Society for Promoting Christian Knowledge
36 Causton Street
London SW1P 4ST
www.spckpublishing.co.uk

Published in the United States by Baker Academic
a division of Baker Publishing Group
P.O. Box 6287, Grand Rapids, MI 49516-6287
www.bakeracademic.com

British Library Cataloguing-in-Publication Data
A catalogue record for this book is available from the British Library

Library of Congress Cataloging-in-Publication Data is on file at the Library of
Congress, Washington, D.C.

SPCK ISBN 978–0–281–05953–9
eBook ISBN 978–0–281–06493–9

Baker Academic ISBN 978–0–8010–4539–4

Typeset by Graphicraft Limited, Hong Kong
First printed in Great Britain by Ashford Colour Press
Subsequently digitally printed in Great Britain

Produced on paper from sustainable forests

For
Anca and Andreas
τὸ μυστήριον τοῦτο μέγα ἐστίν

Contents

Illustrations

Figures

Table

Preface

It is now 25 years since I first used this little work, the *Didache*, as a core text in teaching. Over the years I have used it in almost every conceivable context where the teaching of theology takes place. I have used it with university undergraduates, in seminaries and convents, supervised dissertations devoted to it, used it at gatherings of ministers of various denominations and read it with groups of ordinary Christians in real communities. I have taken it into the pulpit, and most recently prepared a course upon it that will be delivered over the internet! Yet I am still fascinated by it and, more importantly, every group with whom I have worked through this text has found it fascinating. The *Didache* has an ability to change a leisurely class quietly studying Christian texts into a group eager to ask basic questions about Christianity and about its structures and practices, to spur them on to investigate what we know about early Christianity, and to empower them to look afresh at long-familiar texts and assumptions. I think this ability to make people sit up and start looking with a new energy at Christian origins comes from the text's unique combination of familiarity – people recognize so much of its contents from reading the Gospels or just from the practices they see in their churches – and unfamiliarity – this teaching is not presented in the way that it is found in the New Testament's texts nor do the practices conform with the deeply held assumptions of many churches. This mix of the well known with the startlingly different makes people sit up and look with new eyes both at the past and the present. It is this sense of the *Didache* as a text that can excite us that I have tried to convey in this book.

Over the years I have often been asked for a 'guide book' to the *Didache* that would be more than a summary introduction, yet not a full-blown academic commentary (and there are several excellent ones), that would allow its reader to reread the *Didache* and draw more out of its text. I told many of those groups that I would write such a book but kept delaying putting pen to paper. Now, at last, here it is. If any of those many people with whom I have read the *Didache* over the years picks up this book, that person will find much that is familiar, but may also find a question they remember someone raising in class, or a comment first heard in a seminar. I have learned more about the text each time I have gone through it with a group; and I am thankful for all the discussions, questions, comments but, especially, my students' enthusiasm.

Thomas O'Loughlin
Nottingham

Acknowledgements

Over the years I have incurred numerous debts for help in understanding and appreciating the *Didache*, not just among my academic colleagues, but, more significantly, among students with whom I have read this text.

I would like to single out two students for special mention, Valerie Warren and Joy Powell, because they were the first to force me to search out how looking at the earliest churches could be a valuable part of the theological enterprise today. Over the years I can also recall very many conversations with colleagues on either the text as a whole or specific aspects of it. I hope they have as pleasant a recollection of the meal or the meeting in the pub when they suggested something, now incorporated here, as I have. I would also like to single out a few of my colleagues whose conversation over many years has helped me to clarify my views, especially Professors Robert Jewett, Seán Freyne, Justin Taylor and D. P. Davies, and Drs Kieran O'Mahony and the late Michael Maher, *requiescat in pace Domini*. I would also like to express my gratitude to Drs Frances Knight and Francisca Rumsey for acting as sounding boards for the book as it stands, and particularly to the latter for proofreading the text and saving me from more than one blunder! The positions taken, and the remaining imperfections, are, however, my own.

Working with SPCK has been a most pleasant experience: its staff were enthusiastic from the start, and have been the very model of generosity in their patience for the completed text. As ever, I have built up debts among many librarians, but Kathy Miles and Neil Smyth have been unfailing in their ready help.

Introduction

Why the *Didache*? Why bother to write a book about such a text, and why bother to read such a book? Let me try to answer these questions by way of an introduction to this book.

One might expand the question and ask why should a Christian read any ancient text, be it a Gospel, a letter from an early Christian leader, or the *Didache*? My answer is in three overlapping parts. First, members of every religious community – big or small – are always engaged in a process of forgetting some aspects of their past while simultaneously remembering and giving new life to other aspects of their past. The forgetting is sometimes the necessary jettisoning of attitudes that they recognize as no longer appropriate. Take slavery as an example. Christianity emerged in a culture where slavery was an accepted part of the social structures and the only concern was that owners treat their slaves 'as brothers in the Lord'. The very notion that one could be a 'brother' Christian and a slave seems ludicrous to us; yet Christians defended slavery as an institution until well into the nineteenth century!

But we also forget 'by accident' and usually this happens when we take a familiar form of any practice and imagine that either it was 'always like this' or that 'it cannot be other than like this'. Take, for instance, the arguments that go on interminably between Christian denominations about the Eucharist – very often the most minor details of practice are considered 'essentials'. Yet often, all sides in the dispute have forgotten that this gathering is a meal, and a meal in which Christ is present among the disciples gathering in his name. But this fundamental aspect has been forgotten because a real meal was socially awkward in the highly stratified society of the second century: they had forgotten that part of the message of the meal was that the Christian community was to cut through such social divisions. Recalling these forgotten aspects can teach us humility before the past, the dangers of just repeating practice, and that there are aspects of Christian practice that we need to recover. But remembering can also be dangerous: when we remember bits and pieces at random, we sometimes can get the wrong end of the stick! Take the notion, very common among some churches (mainly in north America) that suddenly, sometime soon, some Christians are going to be whisked away into the clouds to be with Jesus – this is referred to as 'the rapture' and presented as Paul's teaching in 1 Thessalonians 4.14–18. But this bit of remembering also forgets that Paul later abandoned this notion; and so it just remained in the memory as a curiosity. Another piece of remembering is that which has rediscovered that sin is not just an individual's personal crimes, but that there is a social dimension to sin as it is portrayed in the Scriptures and our early texts: Christians have to work to build just societies and their own society as 'the Church' must reflect this. But both forgetting and remembering – important keys for Christian tradition – need to be done with conscious interaction with the past and the best way to so interact with earlier Christians is through careful and critical examination of the texts of those Christians. The texts are windows allowing us to see their imaginations of faith.

A second reason for reading early texts is that we are all aware that history does not stand still. Even the most conservative person – who loves to imagine that nothing has changed until now and who hopes that nothing will change in the future – knows that they are getting older (inevitable change) and their younger disciples see things differently (yet more change)! Churches and communities change in their questions, their practices, their ways of presenting faith – and in what worries them. Sometimes change is swift, even dramatic, and then it is very easy to provide pictures of the situation 'before' and 'after' so that the change is clearly visible – although we should note that providing an explanation of why the change came about may be very complex and keep historians busy for centuries. Such moments as the legalization of Christianity by Constantine in AD 313 and the Reformation in the sixteenth century are examples of very clear, major developments – even though we may be unclear as to why they came about then and in that form. But most change in Christian practices and understanding is so gradual as to be invisible. Each generation tries to preserve the past, but makes tiny incremental changes, once here and another time there, so that the final state may have the same name as the first, but be different from its origins in every other respect! Explaining how this present state occurs is best done by looking at its past and seeing how practices have grown and changed over decades and centuries. This is explaining the present, and Christian belief in the present, as the outcome of generations of activity. This explanation is neither a justification of the present nor an approbation of the process: it simply explains and allows for a more informed judgement about the present and the past. Some evolution is wholly necessary and needs to be affirmed; some is corrosive and needs to be corrected, and some is just what happened and studying it can explain some of the strange nooks and crannies of practice that appeal to some, but make others want to go off 'spring cleaning'. In such a study of the present as the outcome of its past, looking at a guide to practice that is as old as the *Didache* has very clear advantages.

The third reason for reading the *Didache* is that Christianity is an explicitly historical religion: it is based on a historical individual, Jesus, and what he did and taught. Christianity is also the community descended from the community that Jesus formed around himself: it treasures its past and its memories. Whenever Christians gather they almost invariably look backwards to that time by reading the stories (our four Gospels) produced by and for the second generation of Christians so that they could look back to Jesus. It was that second generation of Christians that used the *Didache*. So looking backwards as a valuable activity in discipleship is a mainstay of Christianity, and the *Didache* is a book about the details of discipleship in that generation. This historical dimension of Christianity, which lies at the heart of the attention given by Christians to the Scriptures in both liturgy and study, is all too often ignored in our intense quest to know what those scriptural books 'mean' as if they were books of wisdom written by philosophers rather than books produced in the churches to help us in the task of historical remembering. It is worth recalling these words by the great French historian Marc Bloch (1992, p. 4):

> Christianity is a religion of historians. Other religious systems have been able to found their beliefs and their rites on a mythology nearly outside human time. For sacred books, the Christians have books of history, and their liturgies commemorate, together with episodes from the terrestrial life of a God, the annals of the church and the lives of the saints.

Because Christians are always recalling those first churches and their memories, this text, the *Didache*, is precious. It gives us insight into how those communities came into being, how they viewed themselves, and their practice as disciples. To study it is to look afresh at the very core of our Christian memory.

Two final notes. First, the *Didache* came to the attention of scholars almost a century and a half ago, and since then there has been no shortage of scholarly books upon it. This book does not seek to compete with them, but to introduce the text. Because of its introductory nature I have not put in footnotes and have kept references to a minimum. At the end of the book is a guide to further reading, and on particular points that readers might want to follow up I have placed references in brackets with this sign, >, followed by a name, which means: if you want to know more about this point, go to that book/ article whose details are listed under 'Further reading'. Second, the Greek word *didache* means 'teaching'/'training' – an activity (often distinguished from 'proclamation': *kerugma*) – but it is also the title of this text: 'The Teaching' or 'The Training'. When it is the activity that I am referring to, I spell it '*didache*' (lower-case initial letter), and when I am referring to the ancient text, I spell it '*Didache*'.

1

A chance discovery

It's the stuff of scholars' dreams and the plot of a hundred films. A young library-bound academic turns over the leaf of an ancient manuscript and there, there before his eyes, is a long-lost text. People had heard of it and wondered about it, but now, without a doubt, he has found it. It is a eureka-moment. The scholar's life will change: from obscurity behind bookshelves he will become world famous. Indeed, the whole discipline will be changed by his discovery. What has he found in this ancient hand-written codex? A booklet used in the very first decades of his religion. It is older than most of his religion's most famous records, and gives a completely new slant on how its adherents lived their lives, saw themselves and expressed their beliefs. It is a short text, and deceptively simple, but it will cause an earthquake that will shake thousand-year-old certainties, beginning a revolution that changes the way a world-wide religion looks at its most august books and thinks about its own origins. The only element from the movies that is missing in this story is that of a secret plan to hide the discovery and destroy the evidence! It seems too bizarre to be true, but that, in a nutshell, is the story of the discovery of the *Didache* in 1873.

Philotheos Bryennios was born in Constantinople (Istanbul) in 1833 (see Figure 1.1 overleaf). His family, who lived in a Greek and Christian suburb of what was then the capital of the Ottoman Empire, was very poor but they managed to obtain some basic education for their son, and this allowed him to become the leader of the singing in his local church. There, he

PHILOTHEOS BRYENNIOS.

Figure 1.1 Engraving of Bryennios
This engraving of Bryennios is from the frontispiece of Philip
Schaff's *The Oldest Church Manual called The Teaching of the
Twelve Apostles*, published in New York in 1885; this was the first
scholarly study of the *Didache* in English.

came to the attention of a local bishop – who later became patriarch – who, no doubt noting ability, sponsored his entry into the seminary on the island of Halki just outside Constantinople in the Sea of Marmara. By the age of 23 Bryennios's abilities as a scholar were clearly seen by his superiors for they then took the unusual step of sending him to Germany for training in the latest scholarly methods. This education was paid for by a Greek banker, George Zariphe, who no doubt had been asked to sponsor this young man because he was so promising, and without this gentleman's generosity to theological education we would all be so much poorer! So off Bryennios went, and attended courses in Leipzig, Berlin and Munich (> Schaff, 1885).

Why was this so significant? In the nineteenth century very few Orthodox clerics would have been exposed to the new methods in historical investigation that were being pioneered in Germany at that time. In German universities the long-held views about the amount of information we had on the origins of Christianity were being questioned; the historical worth of the Gospels was being debated; and new standards were being set in the rigour of historical enquiry in theology. Moreover, on the technical side of historical enquiry, these universities were setting new standards in the way that ancient texts were edited – our standard edition of the New Testament in Greek, Nestle-Aland, still bears the name of one of these German pioneers: Eberhard Nestle (1851–1913) – and German scholars were no longer content with just looking at what had been handed down, but were actively seeking new evidence for the history of Christianity through archaeology and through searching obscure libraries for ancient, forgotten treasures. A man typical of this new spirit was Konstantin von Tischendorf (1815–74) who spent the years 1840 to 1860 searching libraries in Europe and the Near East for ancient manuscripts of the Scriptures that might throw light on the origins of the New Testament or help solve problems with its texts. His greatest discovery came in 1844 when he found in the Monastery of St Catherine – in the middle of the Sinai desert – the Codex Sinaiticus which is one of the oldest books we still have that contains the whole of the New Testament, along with the Old Testament, and a few other ancient Christian writings. Our image of Christian origins was changing with each new discovery – and the German universities were leading the advance (> McKendrick, 2006). Tischendorf became a professor in Leipzig in 1859: did Bryennios meet him, hear him, or had he moved on from Leipzig by then? We shall never know, but the young man from the East would certainly have heard of the discoveries in ancient libraries and he clearly imbibed the new spirit of enquiry and learned its careful and meticulous methods.

After just four years in Germany, at the beginning of 1861 Bryennios was summoned back home by the patriarch – who earlier as a bishop had spotted his promise – and made professor of church history at Halki and soon afterwards ordained a presbyter. Then in 1867 he was moved to the seminary in the Phanar district of Constantinople as director. Phanar was a suburb where there were many church institutions and their libraries: Bryennios had rich pickings on his doorstep. Between 1867 and 1875 when he became Bishop of Serrae (and after 1875 his time was mainly taken up with being a bishop and acting as a representative of the patriarch) he not only ran the large seminary but also searched the manuscripts of the libraries around him with the aim of finding better texts of the earliest Christian writers. The first fruits of this search were published in 1875 in Constantinople and were editions of two ancient letters which we call *1 Clement* (a late first-/early second-century letter; > Gregory, 2006) and *2 Clement* (a second-century homily; > Parvis, 2006) but which were then thought to be the work of St Clement who was a bishop in Rome.

It was during this period, probably in 1873, that Bryennios, while working in the library of the Constantinople house of the Monastery of the Holy Sepulchre (Jerusalem) on a manuscript written in AD 1056, found the *Didache*. However, rather than a burst of publicity, Bryennios took his time: he let the significance of what he had found sink in, then he carefully prepared an edition, and his discovery finally became public in Greek in 1883. Within months the work was being published in German, French and English (> Schaff, 1885). A facsimile of the manuscript's text appeared in 1887 (> Harris, 1887), and, after that, the *Didache* was public property.

So how had he found it? It would be nice to have a romantic story of a codex covered in dust or hidden in some secret place or lost and stumbled upon by accident! Alas, the manuscript was well known for other early Christian texts it contains, but no one had gone carefully through the whole book and looked at everything with care! Other scholars went to check on what they already knew about; Bryennios, by contrast, looked at whole codex carefully and was willing to be surprised – there is surely a moral there for every student of the early Church.

What is 'The *Didache*'?

The title, 'The *Didache*', comes from the heading Bryennios found at the head of the short text in the manuscript. It reads *Didache kuriou dia tōn dōdeka apostolōn tois ethnesin* which translates literally as 'the Lord's teaching to the nations through the twelve apostles'. Moreover, it is the same title as that referred to in ancient writers who mention that there was a book with this title used by the earliest Christians. But, as we shall see later, this long title was probably added to the text later – originally it was just called 'the *Didache*'. But saying that 'the *didache*' means 'the teaching' does not take us very far because almost every Christian book ever written could be described as 'a book of teaching' in one way or another. Equally, a quick look through the text does not tell us much either. There are sections that deal with what Christians should and should not do, guidance on prayer and fasting, information on baptism and on what should be said when Christians gather to eat together; there are rules and regulations on how the community should relate to other groups of Christians; and there is a little homily on the return of Christ. It seems more like an album of bits than a single literary creation.

When it was first found this sense of a jumble of discrete items of information reminded scholars of later collections of Church law and so they saw it as a very simple set of guidelines for clerics. So they called it a manual – thinking in terms of the manuals that digested the training of nineteenth-century clergy into handy rules – and so they referred to it as 'a manual of church discipline' or the 'earliest church order'. After all, it is the church officials that are concerned with communicating rules, teaching, and inculcating morality! But there were many problems with this view. Not least, this assumes that the earliest churches had the level of organization that we only see developing much later and that they used a distinction between 'ministers' and 'laity' that was formalized only after several centuries. Moreover, the *Didache* assumes that its teaching is for all Christians, the whole Church in a particular place, and that its information affects everyone within it. However, one stills sees it referred to as both a 'church order' and as a 'manual', even though these are not helpful descriptions as they presuppose late nineteenth-century ways of viewing the early Church.

Another view – found during most of the twentieth century in one way or another – was to assume that, as Christianity spread from synagogue to synagogue and from place to place, the new gatherings of followers of 'the Way' needed guidelines and advice on how they should organize themselves for their community meals – we will see later that these are the kind of meals Paul is referring to in 1 Corinthians 11.17–26 when he reminds the Corinthians that they must eat in a Christian way at the Christian meal – and advice on other matters. For example, they had to know about the Christian discipline of prayer three times a day. Moreover, they had to know the importance of the Christian way of acting, and for this reason (particularly if they were not familiar with Jewish ways of teaching morality) might be glad of a short text of the 'Two Ways' (i.e. 'the Way of Life' and 'the Way of Death'). So what is the *Didache* according to this view? It is a folder of useful information for early churches: information that they found valuable in helping them to get themselves organized. Then, for us, it is a window to their communities; and valuable as a source of background information on the communities that first heard the gospel or who received letters from St Paul. Not only is this the most common approach to the *Didache* but also, since most of the people who read it do so in the context of their studies of the New Testament, the *Didache* becomes a document belonging to 'the Background to the New Testament' and it is read not so much for what the text itself tells us as for what it might tell us about other texts. The problem with this approach (apart from encouraging a view that the *Didache* is only important as 'background' to other ancient writings) is that it does nothing to explain the title. However, we know that the text was always known by the name '*didache*' and we know that it was widely used over a long period (because we have fragments of it in other ancient languages). It was valued and used as containing information that Christians needed – and not just to help them get organized in the first months or years after they became Christians. Whatever else we say about it, we have to explain its title and its extensive use – it is far more than the lucky survival of a set of 'how to' notes.

Up to now we have been speaking of the reception of the *Didache* by those who were excited by the prospect of getting background to the texts of the New Testament or who saw it as fresh historical evidence on how the earliest churches organized themselves. But excitement was far from total: it also produced 'allergic reactions' among those whose views of the early Church or early Christian preaching were most upset by it. Indeed, we can formulate this little rule of thumb: the more that any group bases their current practice on the assertion that they are doing/preaching what was done by either Jesus or the apostles the more they will be antagonized by the *Didache*. We see this illustrated in the two main groups which argued in the late nineteenth and early twentieth centuries that the *Didache* was either a very late document or else a peripheral document.

On the one hand, there were many Roman Catholic scholars who found one part of the *Didache* repulsive: a meal which looked suspiciously like a Eucharist, but which they confidently asserted could not be one as a Eucharist had to have a presbyter and the words of Jesus at the Last Supper for a consecration. They liked the stuff about morality, prayer, fasting and an option for baptism by sprinkling (here was ancient evidence to use against Protestants and the Orthodox churches of the East), but they spilled gallons of ink telling people that the meals were something *other than* the Eucharist. They were certain of this because what the Council of Trent in the sixteenth century had said was infallible, and so it could not be contradicted by a fact – the fact was wrong! This led these scholars into a further conundrum: if the text was early, then it was far harder to claim it as deviant; if it was late, then it was far harder to explain all its early features. The solution was to imagine that in the early churches there were two types of meal: there were boisterous meals that were called 'Eucharists' (as we see in 1 Cor. 11) and there were boisterous meals that were called 'agapes' (love feasts) as we see in the *Didache* and Jude 12. So that was that! However, there was also a tendency to date it as late as possible (they opted for a second-century date) and as far from the mainstream as possible (either Syria or Egypt – but certainly not around the Aegean or in Italy). We might find this sort of special pleading – hammering facts to fit with existing dogma-driven views of the past – amusing; but the legacy of years of books expressing these views without comment is still with us. Within the last few years I have seen an 'explanation' of why the *Didache* does not have 'an institution narrative' (i.e. the words 'this is my body . . .') where the author does not realize that historical study has moved on and we now know that these words only entered the Prayer of Thanksgiving in the fourth century (> Ligier, 1973; > Taft, 2003). Alas, it is very hard to get confused ideas out of the bloodstream of a religion.

The other group who found the *Didache* repulsive were extreme Protestants. While these welcomed 'the omission' of the words of Jesus that were disturbing Catholics – to them it showed that Roman Catholic teachings were not historically demonstrated – they found the prescription of fasting on fixed days (Wednesdays and Fridays) clear evidence that the Church that used the *Didache* was already corrupt and in need of reformation. Fasting had been one of the explosive points during the sixteenth century: it was a 'work' which implied that works could purchase or obtain 'righteousness'. As such, it was a denial that justification came 'by faith alone'; and abandoning fixed days of fasting and abstaining from meat was often the public sign that a town or city had abandoned Catholicism and embraced the Reformation. Now it had been known from the writings of Tertullian (*c.*AD 160–*c.*225) that by the third century this practice of fasting on Wednesdays and Fridays was widely established, but this had been explained by the presence even in the early centuries of a virus called 'Early Catholicism' – taken from the German term, *Frühkatholizismus*, and used as a technical term (> Smith, 1990). But if the *Didache* was as early as the time of the New Testament, then the virus was there even before the death of the last 'inspired writer' – and that would not do! So how was the circle to be squared? It was a deviant and late document, possibly a historical forgery, but it was fully infected with the virus that would only be expelled after it had wholly corrupted the Christian body. So this group described the *Didache* as 'the spoiled child of criticism' (implying that New Testament scholars were wasting their time when they looked to it for background) and argued that it dated from the late third or fourth century (implying that its 'early' features were fraudulent reconstructions). Again, these views became so widespread that many books opted for the 'safe' position and said the *Didache* 'might be as late as the fourth century'. The sad fact is that because this little comment appeared in a widely used textbook for theology students – and because textbooks tend to copy textbooks – one still finds it in students' essays half a century after most scholars gave up trying to show that the *Didache* was a post-first-century document! As we have noted already: confused ideas can have a very long shelf life!

Apprenticeship

To answer the question properly about what the *Didache* is, we must start by looking at what we think it means to call someone 'a Christian'. If one thinks of this as primarily an individual's option (as it is for most people today) then one picks Christianity because one likes some of its ideas, because one thinks them true, or one likes what Christians do. If this is one's model for being a Christian, then 'the teaching' you would want is about what Christians believe or the 'teachings of Jesus' – and there are umpteen books today that are catechisms of just this sort. However, if you think that Jesus came to form a new people, to establish a group, to show a way that people as a community (and not just as a collection of individuals) can go 'to the Father', then how the group is to behave, and how you as a member of the group should behave, becomes as central to being taught to be a Christian as knowing the stories about Jesus. We may not like this 'church-centred' approach, but that is our cultural choice, not a reflection of early Christian living.

Jews in Jesus' time saw themselves as a people, the chosen people of the covenant, the children of Abraham, a community set among the 'nations' – and it was the whole people who were loved by God, and the individual's task was to be a worthy member of the people, a worthy inheritor of the promises made to the patriarchs. Within this community came Jesus who announced a new way of living the covenant: this was his new testament, and a new relationship of the community to the Father. Now the people could address God as *our* Father – note that Christians still pray, in an individualist age, to *our* Father not to *my* Father – and rejoice and thank God for his goodness in sending them the Christ. Soon the followers of Jesus realized that this new way of being the people of God did not just include the Jewish people but could include people 'from every tribe and tongue and people and nation' (Rev. 5.9 [RSV]) and all could become part of this new family of Abraham (Rom. 4) through Jesus. So what does it mean 'to become a Christian'? In a context like this 'being a believer' is more akin to seeking to join a community rather than simply giving assent to a set of teachings or expressing a personal preference. Equally, the act of 'joining the Christians' is not simply 'a moment of conversion' – remember Paul described his conversion moment as exceptional (> 1 Cor. 15.8; and Eph. 3) – nor was it just the moment of baptism: to join this new community took time. One had to learn how to live this new lifestyle, one had to be shaped and formed, one had to be gradually initiated into its values and activities, as well as its beliefs. This was more like joining a group where there is an apprenticeship, one learns slowly by learning to belong, and one has to show the group that one's initiation is taking place. The *'didache'*/the 'teaching' means not what one downloads in a moment or in a classroom, but what we would call 'the training' that one needs to absorb before one is fully one of the 'chosen race, a royal priesthood, a holy nation, God's own people, that you may declare the wonderful deeds of him who called you out of darkness into his marvellous light' (1 Pet. 2.9 [RSV]). Just as apprentices have to spend time before being accepted fully into the group of skilled workers and have to show that they have mastered the skills common to the group – they have 'done the training' – so people becoming Christians had to have mastered the training on how the group lived. Put another way: they had to have absorbed the *didache* (> Milavec, 2003, pp. 51–172)!

So the *Didache* was not specialist information for just the leaders – a sort of specialists' crib – but something every Christian should know. We will see this again and again as we go through the text: whether it is knowing what are the list of things to do and to avoid, prayers, or group policy on visiting experts – this was the common property of the whole community and it was expected that everyone knew how to act in these circumstances because they had learned the Church's ways during the period of initiation. While apprentices they were formed and shaped as Christians; then, when ready, they entered the group, entered the Christ, at their baptism.

Indeed, there is evidence not only that the *Didache* was intended as a guide for forming those wanting to belong to a church but also that it was intended to be committed to memory. We should bear in mind that there are elements of the *Didache* such as the Two Ways and the Lord's Prayer that were certainly intended for learning by rote (most Christians today can still recite the Lord's Prayer by heart) and that in earlier times people used their memories far more than we do who have ready access to recording devices, whether a pencil and paper or a computer. It was not unusual for people to learn off many long texts so that they could use them when they were far from books: Psalms, hymns and lists of various sorts were all items that a 'well stocked mind' just had available from memory – and it was not considered a great feat to be able to use these without a book. Then there were specialists who could commit whole books to memory and use them to entertain or instruct – people who had learned great long stories and could perform them when needed. We might think of these storytellers as those who could recite the tales from Homer (the equivalent to actors who have learned off Shakespeare's plays), but the same skills were needed by those who could announce the gospel – we shall meet this group later: 'the evangelists' – and who could arrive in a church and recite the whole story of Jesus. So the idea of having the whole of the *Didache* in the memory is not as daunting as it sounds; and the whole text is phrased in such a way that it facilitates commitment to memory (> Milavec, 1994).

So what is 'the teaching'? It is basic information about the Christian group's lifestyle and their activities as the New People on the Way of Life. Once one had absorbed this teaching one had finished one's own apprenticeship and was ready to enter fully into the body of Christ. Then, having mastered the teaching, one was in a position, without needing books or anything else, to act as a mentor in the process of shaping others as apprentice Christians. The *didache* was not just for teaching classes or for teachers, it was not just a set of lessons, it was meant to be absorbed so that its possessor would function as a part of Christ (> Rom. 12) and help others to join 'the Way' (> Acts 9.2).

Why is the *Didache* important?

Over the past 125 years the *Didache* has been studied in all sorts of ways and been used – usually as a supporting document – by biblical scholars, historians of the early Church, liturgists and those who examine how Christian theology has grown and changed over the centuries. And while each group might highlight the importance of the *Didache* in their own way because it throws light on this or that theme which they consider important, we can pick out three more general reasons why it is worth studying this short text – remembering that it only takes between 20 and 30 minutes to read the whole text.

Probably the most common reason why someone today picks up a book like this on the *Didache* is that they have already been studying the collection of early Christian writings that we now refer to as 'the New Testament'. We know that these were addressed to, and first heard by, the churches around the Mediterranean world and we naturally would like to know as much about that audience as we can. The more we know about the audience's situation, and all those factors we lump together under the label 'context', the more our understanding is enhanced. This is an aspect of biblical studies that has been transformed out of all recognition in the last few generations. Our knowledge today of 'context' is so much richer than that of the period before 1950 that earlier books of exegesis are now redundant. We have had the great discoveries of the Dead Sea Scrolls and of the Nag Hammadi Library, but we have also had advances in the study of the place of religion in Graeco-Roman society, how that society worked, and how different religious groups lived side by side in its cities (> Meeks, 2003). When we talk about 'the church in Corinth' we now have a far clearer picture of what we mean, we know much about what was important to that group, and can make sense of many of the remarks of Paul about the conduct of its members that were opaque to earlier readers. But with all these advances in our knowledge it is the earlier discovery of the *Didache* that alone shows us, from the inside, a church organizing itself. The more we learn, the more we understand the *Didache*; and the more important the *Didache* becomes as our most detailed insight into the life of those early churches.

A second reason many people study the *Didache* is a special refinement of the notion of context. When we set aside the Gospels and Acts, most of the documents that we have from the first and early second centuries are letters: those of Paul; those attributed to Paul; then those linked with the names of James, Jude, John, Peter; then the letter to the Corinthians we call *1 Clement*; and then the letters of Ignatius of Antioch. Letters were links between churches; their exchange formed the network that formed 'the Church' out of the churches. The problem with most letters is that they belong to conversations: they either expect an answer or are given as an answer to an earlier letter – and we know that those that have survived are only a fraction of those that were sent. Frequently, when we are reading Paul we have to try to guess what questions he is trying to answer, what the problems were about which his guidance was being sought, or what had annoyed him within a church that caused him to pick up his pen. So reading these letters is often like overhearing one side of a long telephone conversation. We try to make sense of what we hear, but we do not know what the other end is saying: sometimes it is clear what is being said at the other end, sometimes we can have a good idea, but often we can only guess. The *Didache* shows us some of the standard concerns of these churches: from issues of lifestyle, to the importance of eating together, to the problem of visiting preachers who are really just seeking an easy life. Here is a little example. In 2 Thessalonians 3.10 we have a comment by Paul which seems somewhat strange. After making a point of the fact that he paid for his own food while with them, he says: 'For even when we were with you, we gave you this command: if any one will not work, let him not eat' (RSV). The last command seems both harsh and not a little moralistic. Why is this an issue for Paul – had he not better things to be worried about? However, we know from the *Didache* that there were wandering Christians known as 'apostles and prophets' going from church to church, and one of the problems was telling the genuine prophets from those who were using the gospel for their own ends. So the *Didache* sets up a test: unless there is a special need, they must only stay for one day as guests; but, if they stay three days, they are false prophets! To a poor community this rule provided for welcome – and allowed them to hear the apostles but also made sure that they were not exploited (*Did.* 11). Now we can understand Paul. He was demonstrating his authenticity in that he did not exploit his hosts, but earned his own keep. Moreover, he endorses the very same rule: no work, no food!

While not wishing to downplay these 'contextual' reasons for reading the *Didache*, if we just read it for what it tells us about other documents, and not for what it tells us itself about Christianity, then we are missing out on a whole stratum of early Christian wisdom. We have Gospels which tell us the good news that was announced, we have letters that show us how Christians were formulating their beliefs, we have Acts which shows us how they imagined their world-wide activity, and in the *Didache* we see their approach to day-to-day living as Christians. It presents us with a string of insights into what they considered to be the important issues that 'had to be got right' if they were to be disciples on the Way of Life. Some of these aspects are still with us and reading the *Didache* can be a way of refocusing on what is really at issue beneath centuries of encrustation. Some are long gone and now meaningless, but others, though long forgotten, are aspects of Christianity that are worth looking at afresh. Jesus preached and formed a people – and the people formed by the *Didache* were only a generation later. When we view it in this way, we can see that if this little text is a 'spoiled child' then it repays the attention paid to it.

Christianity is a historical religion. It stakes its basic claim on the historical fact of the birth of Jesus in history, the community he founded is the basis of later communities, and his good news lives within the vagaries of human history. As communities in history we are always forgetting bits of what it is to be Christian, while discovering other implications of discipleship. In this process of seeing what we might have forgotten, or being inspired to grow in new ways, studying our past is a central and core activity. Henry Ford said that 'history is bunk' and someone else passed over history as simply 'prologue'; but, for Christians, history is revelation. If Christians are to understand today, we must remember yesterday. Or, as Cardinal Newman put it:

> [T]he history of the past ends in the present; and the present is our scene of trial and to behave ourselves towards its various phenomena duly and religiously, we must understand them; and to understand them, we must have recourse to those past events which led to them. Thus the present is a text and the past its interpretation. (Newman, 1890, p. 250)

For us, looking backwards is a help to understanding Christianity today and tomorrow, and the more ancient the discipleship we examine the more it is likely to throw our activity into relief. And because Christians spend so much of the time debating matters relating to how churches are organized – just look at the energy, indeed venom, that can be expended by a community whenever there is some change in its ritual – looking at a document like the *Didache* can often set matters in perspective. When, today, the Eucharist, and conflicting presentations of 'what it means', can be the issue that divides groups of Christians, it can be thoroughly refreshing to look at the *Didache* where the Eucharist is what keeps people together – and which, incidentally, reveals that most of the quarrels relate to later developments when the Eucharist had changed almost beyond recognition from the meal practice of Jesus and the first churches. In short, the *Didache* is a mirror we can hold up to our practice as members of churches, and let it help us to see ourselves in perspective.

What does the *Didache* show us?

There are many ways that religions could be classified, but a simple one would be to note the relative proportions of interest that a religion gives to the kitchen of an average house and the amount of time it gives to special places such as temples or libraries. Every religion gives some attention to each. It might be that there are food laws or practices at meals or ways of dressing – this is the domestic side of religion and it affects every adherent every day. In this domestic setting religions and life intermingle, and the practices and values are transmitted – almost imperceptibly – to the next generation. Every religion also has special buildings and places – shrines – and major public events, and these need religious specialists: priesthoods. These specialists organize the public events/places and become such a public face for a religion that there is the constant tendency for this public face to appear to be the religion. Then there are the religion's stories: its explanations of what it believes about the world, the world beyond, its tales of origins and purpose. These may become its sacred books – and so there are the experts that interpret them, preserve them, and often turn them into great systems of law and philosophy. The 'kitchen' and the 'temple' are usually distinct, sometimes at loggerheads, but they are mutually dependent and often interact with one another through a calendar: a pattern of practices, fasts and feasts that work over the cycles of time – day, season and year. Christianity is no exception – though in our contemporary world we have a tendency to ignore the kitchen and identify religion with 'going to church'.

This distinction can also help us look at Christian origins. We know quite a lot about the distinction between kitchen and temple in Palestinian Judaism at the time of Jesus – and we know that he laid more emphasis on the 'kitchen' than on the 'temple' aspects of faith. We meet him gathering at meals in houses, walking through the fields, and being very critical about those who were concerned about the 'temple-end' of religion while ignoring the domestic end: become reconciled to a brother before going to offer a sacrifice (*Did.* 14.2/Matt. 5.23–24). Moreover, the first generations of Christians, as they became separate from Judaism, did not have the great public expressions of religions that are well established in societies. They gathered in one another's houses; their central ritual, when they ate together, was very closely related to the kitchen – but evidence for the 'kitchen-end' of religion tends to be ephemeral. And, unlike Judaism, there was no special ritual group: they believed that in Jesus they had all become priests – all could stand in the Father's presence and offer sacrifice – and were 'a priestly people'.

Thus, we have the irony that for a religion that was more kitchen centred than the religion that preceded it or, indeed, than the religion it later became, we have actually little from the kitchen-end of early Christianity. Most of the evidence we have comes from the formal end of religion: we have the great formal stories, the Gospels and the views of the religions' experts, the epistles; but, aside from the *Didache*, almost nothing about the day-to-day structures of this new movement. The *Didache* shows us the disciples living out their Christianity when they were not listening to the Gospels and not hearing great teachers. It may not tell us much about their lives, but is more or less all we have.

Why did the *Didache* disappear?

So if the *Didache* was so valuable in the shaping of early Christians why did it disappear, and why did it not become one of those treasured texts that eventually were seen as the new Scriptures?

Although the *Didache* was discovered by Bryennios in the 1870s, it never really disappeared. This may seem like a contradiction, but can easily be explained by the history of the text.

It is the nature of training texts that they are constantly changing in different tiny ways: bits are added to meet new situations
and bits drop off as no longer relevant. The differences might
hardly be noticed over the period of a year or two, or between
one user and the next, but if you checked on a training manual that had been in use over a long period you would see
major changes. And if this is true in the age of printing which
promotes uniformity, then it is even more true in the age of
manuscripts when each copy was made with a new user in
mind – and it was far easier to add or subtract from a text –
especially a text seen as meeting practical everyday needs. So
it was with the *Didache*: there were probably many ancient
versions, each slightly different, some with more than we have
and some with less. The text was being adapted to new situations, but few would have noticed the incremental changes.
So we see the morality section in many different early Christian
writings – all are related in style, but no two are identical.
We can trace the texts of the eucharistic prayers that we find
in the *Didache* as they evolved to become the more elaborate
prayers of the more formal liturgies of the third and fourth
centuries: they did not stop being used, but changed and
changed until it was hard to recognize that the oak with its
many branches and gnarled trunk started life as a small, smooth
acorn. Then with regard to the regulations, these too became
more complex, and eventually became some of the elements
of canon law. Indeed, once the *Didache* had been found by
Bryennios, it became immediately apparent that most of its
text was known as 'Book VII' in a collection of law from the
later fourth century called the *Apostolic Constitutions*. However,
until Bryennios found the text on its own, we did not realize
that the ancient text whose name we knew was actually
embedded in the *Apostolic Constitutions*. By that time,
Christians did not need to remind each other that they fasted
on Wednesdays and Fridays, because it was so much part
of what was handed down among Christian households that it

was just taken for granted – and its presence in the later book was nothing remarkable.

A far more interesting question is why did Christians abandon the notion of mentoring new members and the notion of there being need for an apprenticeship? The notion of the need for a long initiation did survive for many centuries in the churches. Indeed, the season of Lent is a survival from that practice. It was originally the final period of preparation before baptism – and, as in the *Didache*, this was a period of fasting. Later when baptism was mainly something that happened in infancy, Lent, now no longer needed as a preparation for baptism, evolved its new rationale as a period of penitence (> Talley, 1986). Moreover, as Christianity became more and more an accepted part of society, the notion that one needed an apprenticeship became less and less obvious – and what training there was became something that was more and more in the hands of the religious experts rather than a common task of every member of the church.

When the first Christians set out to preach the good news of Jesus they did so by announcing that 'what had been foretold in the scriptures had come to pass' (> Acts 3.18, for example) in Jesus. Jesus had been born, as written in the prophets (Matt. 2.4–6); he had fulfilled the Scriptures (Matt. 26.54); the Scriptures bore witness to him (John 5.39); he had risen in accordance with the Scriptures (1 Cor. 15.4); then he opened the Scriptures to the apostles so that they could see what the Scriptures said about him (Luke 24.45); and they went out and preached him by 'showing by the scriptures that the Christ was Jesus' (Acts 18.28). So the Christians started off with a large library that they held as sacred – indeed the early Christians held a larger collection of Old Testament books to be 'scripture' than most Christian churches today.

Then there were their own memories: and above all their memory of Jesus, of his life, his teachings, his death and his resurrection. But initially this was a story that was recited among the churches and gradually it became the work of special preachers, evangelists, and their books were not seen as 'scripture' but simply a way of recording the speech of the evangelists. The arrival of an evangelist in a church, or getting a letter from Paul, was an event – and so the memory and its recording on papyrus was kept safely – but it was not until several generations later that these records began to be accorded the status of 'scripture' by parallel with 'the Scriptures' (of the Old Testament). As the second century progressed our four Gospels emerged as the cornerstone of the Church's memory: here was our story and our good news – and by the end of that century they were being accorded a status equivalent to 'the Scriptures'. Around this time the various letters of Paul and other apostles, which had been circulated from the start (> Col. 4.16), also came to have a special status, then the Acts of the Apostles and Revelation were added along with a few other texts here and there. It was only in the fourth century that the notion of a 'canon of the New Testament' really took hold. But by then, there had been umpteen versions of the *Didache*: it was not the sort of document that was held as precious but simply useful. It was used and used, but it never got the extra cachet of being the work of an apostle or evangelist. It is the fortune of all such useful training texts that they did not make it into libraries. Think of how many training manuals you have received over the years: it might have been a ring binder you got for a course; it might have been your notes which were priceless in their day; or it might have been a guide to how to run a computer. Where are they now? In a sense they are still with you – you have absorbed their contents and/or you have got more recent versions. But would you put them with your books in a bookcase? It was the same with the *Didache*: it did its job, but it was valued only for its use; the Gospels and epistles were valued not only for their use in the liturgy but also for their famous associations. There must have been many training manuals in use among the early Christians – we see only reflections of them in the canonical collection, but they did their duty: they formed the communities that heard and valued the gospel.

Gospel and *didache*

We have just been contrasting the *text* of the *Didache* with the *texts* of the four Gospels, so this is an appropriate point to introduce the difference between training/teaching (in Greek called *didache*) and the good news/gospel that is proclaimed/ announced (in Greek called *kerugma*). The distinction can be seen in this way: you rejoice at the announcement (*kerugma*) that God loves us and is sharing his life with us in Jesus; then, having chosen to follow Jesus, you learn how to be a disciple and how to live in a Christian community – this is *didache*. The gospel is the treasure: it tells what God has done, is doing, and has promised; the 'teaching' spells out the implications. Without the good news, Christianity would be just another set of rules and rituals: without the training it would be lovely words in our ears but it might never inform living. *Kerugma* and *didache* are two sides of the same coin. Moreover, we often refer to 'the *kerugma*' meaning the content of the announce- ment of the gospel – in its shortest form this is the confession 'Jesus is Lord' (> 1 Cor. 12.3) – and to 'the *didache*' meaning all the teaching/lifestyle that has to be imbedded in one's life if one is to live as a disciple. We see the two ideas in this early piece of pastoral wisdom: 'preach the word [i.e. the *kerugma*], be urgent in season and out of season, convince, rebuke, and exhort, be unfailing in patience and in teaching [i.e. the *didache*]' (2 Tim. 4.2 [RSV]).

It is this distinction that explains why the text we are going to look at does not contain any stories about Jesus, nor parables, nor even his words laid out as such. All that belongs to the *kerugma*. Our text has a far more down-to-earth purpose: if you have heard the good news, now you must make it a part of your life. We today make a distinction between 'discipleship' and 'discipline'; the first is a life-long endeavour, the second is rules and regulations. For the early Christians there was no such division: the *Didache* was concerned with the discipline – if you knew its demands, you were on the Way because this was what a disciple manifested.

Where and when

A favourite occupation of scholars is trying to tie down exactly where and when ancient documents were written. Indeed, they often pursue the task in such a way that they imagine they can get to a 'place and date' that is parallel to what we find in a modern bibliography. The *Didache* was compiled in Greek and is found in fragments of numerous languages: so wherever it was written it obviously had wide appeal. However, if it had such appeal, then it was found useful in many places – and, therefore, attempts to isolate its place of origin are fruitless! The alternative is to say that it belongs to the Graeco-Roman world or the Mediterranean world – but the same can be said about every early Christian document. So why does one find references in books saying that the *Didache* 'may have originated in Syria' and others saying it 'might have come from Egypt', or others which say that it 'might have appeared in Egypt or Syria'? Egypt was favoured by many early students of the *Didache* as there were no New Testament documents associated with Egypt and it was long known that there were Christians in Egypt from the earliest times – so here was a document without a home, so why not say it comes from Egypt! The scholars who adopted this view were mainly Germans.

However, in the Eucharistic Prayer in the *Didache* we have the phrase 'as the broken loaf was once scattered over the mountains and then was gathered in . . .' (*Did.* 9.4). This is a reference to a theme in the prophets (> Ezek. 36.4 and Nahum 3.18) that the people have been scattered on the mountains and will be gathered back together by the Christ – and now it is realized in the people gathered at the Lord's table. Some scholars, almost all of them French, read the passage literally, asking where mountains for wheat to grow on were to be found in Egypt. Since there were no such mountains, the prayer had come from somewhere with mountains: Syria! This might look like a piece of fine detective work but, in fact, it is silliness. It was with the messianic images from the Scriptures that the first Christians sought to understand the person and work of Jesus, and hence their use of the prophetic image of the great gatherer of Israel for Jesus. Focusing on 'mountains' as a physical object – as if prayers have to be geographically precise – is an example of 'missing the wood for the trees'.

What is far more important to note is that wherever in the Graeco-Roman world it was compiled, it was a place where the separation of Christians from the larger Jewish community was still taking place. The *Didache* assumes that the followers of Jesus know a great deal about Jewish ways and have few problems with them; but at the same time it is anxious to assert the distinctiveness of the Way of Jesus. Most of those who used the *Didache* were not yet a distinct religion, they seem to have seen themselves as a distinct group within Judaism – but some of their distinctive attitudes were bringing them into ever-greater conflict with their coreligionists.

When the *Didache* first came upon the stage of scholarly attention two dates were proposed. Those who looked at the very early structures and the close relationship to Judaism proposed a first-century date; while those who compared sentences in the *Didache* with similar (but not identical) statements in the Gospel of Matthew argued that it must therefore be later than Matthew, so, if Matthew is late first century, the *Didache* could be early second century. Later, often worried by the doctrinal problems of an early date, some scholars proposed a much later date for the work – third or even fourth century – and that it had 'disguised' itself to make itself look primitive.

The problem with such conspiracy theories is that once uttered they are hard to disprove: and so that late date still sometimes crops up. However, the discovery of the Dead Sea Scrolls in 1948 was the complete answer to the conspiracy theorists. This discovery changed for ever our views of Judaism at the time of Jesus (many argue that it is better to speak of the 'Judaisms' of that time) and our views of the *Didache*.

New scholarship from the 1950s could point positively to a first-century date, indeed one before 70 (> Audet, 1996). Moreover, our understanding of how the Gospels emerged (> Bauckham, 1998) – earlier views tended to imagine the Gospel writers sitting in the equivalent of a study surrounded by the books they were using and writing for a distinct church – meant that it is just as likely that Matthew was using phrases that were in the *Didache* or were in common use (> Garrow, 2004; Draper, 2006a; summary of arguments in Milavec, 2003, pp. 693–739). So the broad consensus today is for a first-century date. This could be as early as 50 (so we could use the *Didache* to give us background for the sort of Christian life being lived in the churches to which Paul was writing) or as late as 80 or 90 (in a church which had welcomed Matthew or was looking forward to his visit). However, while I am adamant about the need to see this as a reflection of the earliest churches – and so a first-century date – I am less concerned with arguments for before/after 70 or before/after Matthew. My reason for this apparent indifference is that training was not uniform – there was no 'central planning office' – nor does every aspect of a group's practice change when the latest book arrives! So when was it in use? In all probability a version of the *Didache* was being committed to memory by groups of followers of Jesus by the middle of the first century – and what we have reflects a very early stage in that text's life and influence. The training would gradually have changed as the churches developed and changed, and in many places, by the early second century, much of what we find in the text would have seemed out of date – and, eventually, much of it would have seemed out of date everywhere. So we study it as a window on the first and second generation of Christians, who were close to the patterns of Jewish faith, seeking to understand the new way of Jesus, Christians who would have known that there were still many alive who had met and heard Jesus, and who belonged to a church that might have longed for a visit by an evangelist and an opportunity to hear his telling of the gospel.

2
Choosing a way

When we start thinking about our lives, where we are now with decisions to make, the past and how through various ups and downs we have arrived here, and then the future, our hopes and desires, we seem to adopt the image of walking along a path as if it is the most natural image in the world. Looking backwards we might say that 'our *path* has been rocky'; in the present we might say that 'we are coming to a fork in the *road* and must make some hard decisions'; and when we are planning we say that 'the *way* ahead looks clear'. The notion of life as walking along a path, indeed walking towards a destination, seems deeply embedded within us. This imagery is also part of the symbolism of many religions. Sometimes we give it an explicitly religious expression as when we compare life to a 'pilgrimage', but often when we simply refer to 'our *way* of life' we have the religious dimension hovering in the background. Using the images of 'way', 'path' or 'road' for our lives we are implicitly invoking the notion that life is about movement, that there is dynamism and freedom with scope for choices. By contrast, other notions can seem static or imply a lack of freedom. The common modern notion of 'lifestyle' is static; it implies that others are determining or appreciating 'our style'; while other images assume that we are passive: simply responding to forces beyond our control. Even the common religious theme of 'vocation' can imply that our task is set from outside us and we just accept it as something imposed. But the image of walking along a 'road' implies that we are moving, looking forward, and can choose where our foot falls next.

Not surprisingly, this notion had been in use in Judaism for centuries (e.g. Jer. 6.16) before the time of Jesus and has played a key role in Christianity from the start: 'These men are servants of the Most High God, who proclaim to you the way of salvation' (Acts 16.17 [RSV]).

The Two Ways

But the word is very near you; it is in your mouth and in your heart, so that you can do it.

See, I have set before you this day life and good, death and evil. If you obey the commandments of the LORD your God which I command you this day, by loving the LORD your God, by walking in his ways, and by keeping his commandments and his statutes and his ordinances, then you shall live and multiply, and the LORD your God will bless you in the land which you are entering to take possession of it. But if your heart turns away, and you will not hear, but are drawn away to worship other gods and serve them, I declare to you this day, that you shall perish; you shall not live long in the land which you are going over the Jordan to enter and possess.

(Deut. 30.14–18 [RSV])

This statement, put by the author into the mouth of the great lawgiver Moses, comes at the dramatic climax of the book of Deuteronomy: all the law has been imparted, the new historical view of the past from the perspective of the Second Temple has been set out, and now, just before his last will and the account of his death, the People of Israel are presented with this choice: the way of covenant which leads to life and rejoicing in good things, the way of death which is the result of choosing another way and ignoring the commandments. Religion as offering humanity a moral choice has never been so dramatically described. And teachers, first Jewish and later both Jewish and Christian, would spend a lot of time fleshing out that final Mosaic challenge.

However, before we look at how that challenge was used in early Christian *didache*, it is worth noting four aspects of that text in Deuteronomy that animated its many follow-ups until well into Christian times when some elements disappeared. First, this presents human goodness and evil as a moral choice. Good comes from good choices and evil from bad choices. This sounds simple, but many ancient cultures saw these outcomes as the result of the whims either of divine beings or of cosmic forces. There is no place here for cosmic fatalism such as the notion that our destiny is written in the stars. In this vision our destiny is in our own hands: we must positively choose good and deliberately avoid evil. This is a commonplace today, but for many people in the Graeco-Roman world it was a liberation from fatalism; and the notion of a religion that gave full scope to moral action (think of alternatives such as religion that is a series of attempts to placate an angry deity) was one of the attractive features of Judaism around the time of Jesus, and an important reason why it was attracting converts who were known as 'proselytes' or 'fearers of God' or 'worshippers of God'.

Second, this is not a challenge that is offered to an individual or a group of individuals: it is offered to a community, a single reality, 'the people'. The individual had to accept the way as a member of the people, but it was the whole community that had to choose to set out on the way to life. Moreover, when individuals abandoned the commandments then the whole community was in jeopardy. We think of morality almost exclusively in individual terms – even when a whole society is led astray by a few individuals – and so find this notion of a 'people of the covenant' hard to appreciate. However, without this awareness of the centrality of community we cannot make sense of much of Jewish and early Christian writings on the Two Ways.

Third, the rules were not there just as an ethical standard: they were there as part of a formal relationship with God – a covenant with promises on both sides. Obedience was presented not as simply adherence to rules but as keeping one side of a bargain within a whole relationship with God. We tend to break religion into 'relationship' and 'rules' – but we cannot understand the *Didache* if we start with such a distinction. The *Didache* can start with a set of rules because these presuppose a relationship: the rules show the parameters of the relationship one is choosing.

Fourth, there are the assumptions that these rules are within our capability, that people can accomplish such a life, that the rules are there for their good, and that they are not there as a kind of test or 'obstacle course' to see who will fall out. God does not set the rules as a way of weeding out the weaklings. This is not an examination but a guide as to how to progress from life to life. And it is assumed that God wants the whole people, and therefore every member of the community, to have life.

Turning the choice presented in the covenant into a list of 'what had to be done' and 'what had to be avoided' became a task for teachers: lists would make the challenge simpler to communicate, easier to remember, and produce a sense of community in the group – everyone could recite the same lists and sense that they were part of a shared project. We have such a list from among the writings found in Qumran – it was used by the community that hid those 'Dead Sea Scrolls' – and we have several early Christian examples apart from that in the *Didache*. Each list is different, yet all are similar. While the lists copy from one another, there probably was no single 'original' of which they are variants. Rather there was the idea of such a list of 'dos and don'ts' and a common stock of moral wisdom, and then different teachers used to a greater or lesser extent an existing list. We have several such lists in early Christian texts and their importance is not that we might find '*the* list' but that they show us the prominent place that was attached to this sort of moral training for those who were entering the community of the new covenant.

In the *Didache* this list of how a member of the church should live takes up just over a third of the whole document. But while the image of 'dos and don'ts' is what strikes everyone on reading the *Didache* for the first time, it is actually a far more sophisticated vision of Christian living than a simple checklist of actions. The *Didache* opens with a choice: on the one hand there is the way of life and on the other hand there is the way of death – you can hear the voice of someone reciting this to his or her apprentice – and there is a great difference between these ways (*Did.* 1.1). And the difference between them is not only in content but in the way they are presented: the 'don'ts' are a list of actions to avoid, but the way of life is presented in a far more all-embracing way: here are the underlying attitudes that must inform particular actions.

The renewed covenant

The 'Way of Life' begins as a statement that we, familiar with the Gospels, imagine in the context of a scene from the life of Jesus:

> And one of them, a lawyer, asked him a question, to test him. 'Teacher, which is the great commandment in the law?' And he said to him, 'You shall love the Lord your God with all your heart, and with all your soul, and with all your mind. This is the great and first commandment. And a second is like it, you shall love your neighbour as yourself. On these two commandments depend all the law and the prophets.'
>
> (Matt. 22.35–40 [RSV])

And before Matthew presented it in this way, Mark had used it in his preaching with different scenery and with a slightly different slant:

> And one of the scribes came up and heard them disputing with one another, and seeing that he answered them well, asked him, 'Which commandment is the first of all?' Jesus answered, 'The

first is, "Hear, O Israel: The Lord our God, the Lord is one; and you shall love the Lord your God with all your heart, and with all your soul, and with all your mind, and with all your strength." The second is this, "You shall love your neighbour as yourself." There is no other commandment greater than these.'

(Mark 12.28–31 [RSV])

But in the *Didache* we get this central piece of early Christian teaching without scenery or comment:

The way of life is this: first, you shall love God who created you; second, your neighbour as yourself; all those things which you do not want to be done to you, you should not do to others.

(*Did.* 1.2)

The so-called 'Golden Rule' is here given just tacked onto the first and second Christian commandments. When this was made into part of the preaching, by Matthew (7.12) and Luke (6.31), it was put into a positive form of what you would like to happen to you, that you should behave like that to others, but here it is just baldly stated as the basis of how the group lives. We are tempted to ask which form was 'original': do *not* do what you would *not* like others to do to you, or act as you would like others to act? But such a question misses the basic point: wisdom consists in appreciating that individuals act within society and the actions of each must be those that build community. Humans are not islands. This means acting as you would want others to act and not acting as you would want others not to act. The community wanted to rejoice in life: that involved acting in life-enhancing ways while rejecting ways that destroyed the peace and harmony of life within the group.

This way of living as God's new people is then spelled out in more detail where the Christian had to act in a way different from the ways that others have acted towards him or her. So 'the teaching' on loving God and neighbour means:

Bless those who curse you;

Pray for those who are your enemies;

Do fasts for those who persecute you.

What benefit is it if you love those who love you? Do not even the gentiles do that? Rather, you must love those who hate you, and so you are not to treat the other person as your enemy.

Abstain from carnal desires.

If someone strikes your left cheek, then turn the right cheek towards him also, and you will be perfect.

If someone makes you go one mile, then go the extra mile with him.

If someone takes your coat, then let him have your jacket.

If someone takes your property, then you are not allowed to ask for it back.

Give to everyone who asks help from you, and do not seek a return because the Father wants his generosity to be shared with everyone.

Blessed is anyone that gives according to this command, for that person goes without punishment. But, watch out for those who received these things: if they receive things from need, then there is no punishment, but if they receive these things without need then they shall have to explain why they acted in that way and they shall be questioned about it when in prison and they will not be released until the last penny is repaid.

But remember it has also been said that 'you should let your gift sweat in your hands until you know to whom to give it'.

(*Did.* 1.3–6)

Again, anyone familiar with the Gospels has heard most of this already. In the Gospels it is presented in various scenes and sermons of Jesus, although the scenes often differ between Luke and Matthew. Some of it can be found elsewhere in the early writings that came to be considered as the New Testament. For example, 'abstain from carnal desires' is found in 1 Peter 2.11: 'Beloved, I beseech you as aliens and exiles to abstain from the passions of the flesh that wage war against your soul' (RSV). The final item about letting your gift sweat in your hands cannot be found exactly in any known scriptural text (the nearest is Ecclus. 12.1) but became a proverb among Christians because Augustine was still quoting it in the early fifth century, assuming that his audience knew it.

Over the years most of the energy devoted to this passage has focused on whether this is (1) a variant of Matthew's Gospel (hence some date the *Didache* after that Gospel), or (2) from the same strand of memory within the Church as that which Matthew incorporated into his preaching (a very common position) or (3) whether Matthew has committed this to memory as *didache* and then woven the teaching known among his audience into his presentation of the good news of Jesus' life, death and resurrection (another common position today). However, this concern about relating the *Didache* to another early Christian text passes over the most striking feature of what this tells us about early Christianity. This teaching about loving and forgiving enemies is not some 'counsel of perfection' or some ideal: it is presented as the ordinary teaching that every Christian had to take as part and parcel of following the Way of Life. Moreover, this was all seen as simply spelling out the first Christian commandment: to love God. Looked at in this way it puts the preaching of the evangelists in perspective: they provide commentary and context; here, in the teaching, it is laid out as the basic demands of discipleship. It also helps us to understand statements like: 'If any one says, "I love God," and hates his brother, he is a liar; for he who does not love his brother whom he has seen, cannot love God whom he has not seen' (1 John 4.20 [RSV]), or 'For this is the love of God, that we keep his commandments. And his commandments are not burdensome' (1 John 5.3 [RSV]).

The *Didache* then moves on to 'the second part of the training' (*Did.* 2.1) which it sees as relating to obeying laws about our conduct with our neighbour:

You shall not murder.
You shall not commit adultery.
You shall not corrupt boys.
You shall not be promiscuous.
You shall not steal.
You shall not practise divination.
You shall not practise with magic potions.
You shall not kill a child in the womb nor expose infants.
You shall not try to take your neighbours' goods.
You shall not perjure yourself.
You shall not act as a false witness.
You shall not speak evil of others.
You shall not hold grudges.
Do not be fickle or deceitful because the deceitful tongue is the
snare of death. (*Did.* 2.2–4)

This is far more familiar teaching: we know most of it as the
Ten Commandments and the additions can be seen as special
instances of the commandments.

For the early community making the choice of the Way was
a choice for a life of moral responsibility where many of the
actions they were to see as sinful – such as divination or seeking
to get magical spells to ward off evil – would have been taken
for granted in the wider culture. The person who was learning
this (the apprentice) from the Christian who was doing the
training is referred to here as 'my child' – a typical expression
in master–disciple training manuals – and told to flee away
from every evil and even 'from everything that looks like it'
(*Did.* 3.1). The 'child' must learn not to be arrogant but humble,
because 'the humble shall inherit the earth' (*Did.* 3.7).

Then the teaching returns to the positive way that a Christian
must live. The disciple must remember the one who is acting
as trainer and give him/her respect because he/she speaks
the word of the Lord, and 'wherever the things of the Lord
are spoken about, there the Lord is present' (*Did.* 4.1). The very
act of learning to be a Christian, and learning the teaching, is

a holy activity that brings student and teacher into the divine presence. Here we see how close is the *Didache* to its Jewish background: to study God's law with a teacher is to come into the divine presence. This is the 'high' view of learning/teaching that was common in Judaism – hence the title of respect, *rabbi*, given to Jesus – and remained so; but all too soon it would be passed over in Christianity. This interest in teaching also extends to the role of parents with children: they must not neglect 'son or daughter, but, from their youth, train them in the fear of the Lord' (*Did.* 4.9). The notion that 'The fear of the Lord is the beginning of knowledge; fools despise wisdom and instruction' is traditional wisdom (> Prov. 1.7, for example), but the idea that training in the Way extends to both son *and* daughter is something new.

Much of this is familiar because it is similar to later Christian teaching. Other aspects are understandable against the background of the larger society – such as the horror of magical practices that had long been seen, within Judaism, as leading to idolatry (*Did.* 3.4) – but some prescriptions still seem strange. While we have a prohibition of grumbling (*Did.* 3.6 and 4.7), a call for people to work honestly with their hands (*Did.* 4.6) and to share everything with a brother in need (*Did.* 4.8), we also have a ban on giving orders to your slaves when angry (*Did.* 4.10) and a call to slaves to be submissive in fear and respect (*Did.* 4.11). Moreover, there is an expectation that individuals would acknowledge their sins in the presence of the community (*Did.* 4.14), a practice that several centuries later would lead to major problems within Christianity (> O'Loughlin, 2000).

Having gone into so much detail on the demands of the Way of Life, the Way of Death is given in summary. All the acts already forbidden ('murders, adulteries . . . acts of idolatry . . . thefts' – *Did.* 5.1) are listed in summary as the steps along the other path. But in this repetition, from the opposite perspective, there is not just the usual list of individual sinful acts, but another reminder of the obligations to the community. Where the Way of Death is followed:

> These people do not know gentleness, they lack patience, they love worthless things and pursue money. These people are without mercy for the poor, and do nothing on behalf of the oppressed.
> These people do not know who was their Maker.
> They are murderers of children, they are corrupters of God's image, they turn away from those in need, oppress the afflicted, are advocates of the wealthy, treat the poor unjustly.
>
> (*Did.* 5.2)

The *Didache* seems to be fully aware of the phenomenon of those who saw morality in terms of the avoidance of specific sinful acts by the individual, while not ignoring the social nature of sin and the social demands that are made on those who seek God. Christians were not to ignore the demands of seeking justice in society and showing a constant concern for the poor, and still imagine that they were not on the Way of Death.

Jesus and the teaching

In reading the Two Ways we are immediately confronted with the difference between the *kerugma* (preaching) and the *didache* (teaching). Here is an example. Most Christians are familiar with this statement: if someone strikes you on the right cheek, turn to him the other also. Indeed, it has been shortened in common parlance to the phrase, 'turning the other cheek', implying that one should not retaliate with violence for violence. If we ask Christians where this statement comes from, and why it is important, the answer will be either that it comes from Jesus and, therefore, deserves some respect; or that it is in the Christians' holy book and as such has authority and deserves respect. So, even if we think turning the other cheek to be a daft idea or pious ideal, the explanation involves the notion of authority. You can find it in the Sermon on the Mount ('But I say to you, Do not resist one who is evil. But if any one strikes you on the right cheek, turn to him the other also': Matt. 5.39 [RSV]) and so it is part of the Christian legacy. However, in the *Didache* none of these demands – and it contains virtually the same contents as the Sermon on the Mount but in a different format – is explained by an appeal to authority. Rather, this is the way of the community of the Christians so that they as a community 'whom the Spirit has prepared' (*Did.* 4.10) can follow the Way of Life. While we seek an explanation for what we find inexplicable and, in effect, disavow the idea by appealing to authority, they took this stance as a basic moral demand flowing from the type of community to which they had committed themselves.

In the teaching (*didache*) the demands of the Way were laid out as a collection of rules. These turned the headline commandment of 'love God and neighbour' into immediate and practical actions, such as avoiding sorcery in one instance of everyday life and turning the other cheek in another. Why does one do this? Because it is part of the package of wisdom of the community of the new covenant: God has set before us two ways, the Spirit has prepared us, and the Lord has come among us, and so these ways of behaving are the implications of the Way of Life. When by contrast the evangelist preached (the *kerugma*) the good news that Jesus is the saviour of the people (> Stanton, 2004, pp. 9–62) he was engaging in a completely different task. Incorporating the same content into the gospel is not simply reiterating the teaching while giving it 'a named source' nor is it attempting to justify the teaching by giving it an authoritative origin (most of it can be found, in any case, within Jewish tradition), but doing something rather different. The teaching was taken for granted: this was the Way of the community, it has been committed to memory, it was the standard by which they sought to live. The evangelist now tells the larger story of the plan of God which reaches back into the history of Israel (e.g. Matt. 1.1–16) and reaches forwards to embrace the whole mission of the people to make disciples of all nations and the end of time (e.g. Matt. 28.20), and at the heart of this plan is the Christ-event: the totality that is the birth, life, teaching, death and resurrection of Jesus. This is the gospel the community rejoice in and celebrate. Part of this preaching of the gospel is to show that Jesus lies at the centre of this great covenant – and one of the ways that this is shown is by demonstrating that his life and teaching is the perfect expression of the covenant's Way of Life. Far from the evangelists linking the teaching to Jesus to give it authority, they link Jesus to the teaching to show who he is as the Anointed of the Father.

Jews and gentiles

Reading the Two Ways we are forcefully struck by how embedded the life of the early Church was within Jewish life and practice at the time and within the vision of life that was the covenant of Israel. This covenant was not yet seen by followers of Jesus as an 'old covenant' (or 'old testament'), rather it was the same covenant, the same promise by God, and the same acceptance of being God's people that was continuing now in their following of Jesus. With Jesus that covenant had reached the new stage of the Messiah (literally: 'the anointed one'; in Greek terminology: 'the Christ') having come among the people. And while we shall note in later chapters that there were tensions between the followers of Jesus and other Jews, the dominant theme in this section of the *Didache* is that the Way of Life required in following the Messiah follows on from the Way of Life that the covenant with Israel demanded. We see this continuity by looking at Jewish texts from before Jesus' time, for example, a short work known as the *Testament of Asher* (> Charlesworth, 1983, vol. 1, pp. 816–17), or by looking at the *Community Rule* from Qumran which is roughly contemporary with Jesus and the *Didache* (> García Martínez, 1994, pp. 6–7). Likewise we find this continuity formally embraced by Matthew when he has Jesus utter these words: 'For truly, I say to you, till heaven and earth pass away, not an iota, not a dot, will pass from the law until all is accomplished' (Matt. 5.18 [rsv]).

However, this group of Christians knows that it is attracting people to the Way for whom the covenant and its demands are something new. We are familiar with this moment in the history of the early Church from Paul's letters where he struggles with those who want to force gentiles who are seeking to become followers of Jesus to take up *all* the demands of the law such as adherence to the dietary laws, and even force men converts to undergo circumcision (> Murphy-O'Connor, 1996, pp. 130–57). This issue of how many of the detailed demands of the covenant are necessary for gentile converts is also present in the *Didache*. For the *Didache* these converts did not have to take on-board all the demands listed in the law and become perfect observers of the law. Rather this is what it calls for:

> Take care that no one leads you astray from this Way of the Teaching, because any other teaching takes you away from God. Now if you are able to bear the whole of the Lord's yoke, you will be complete. However, if you are not able [to bear that yoke], then do what you can.
>
> And concerning food regulations, bear what you are able. However, you must keep strictly away from meat that has been sacrificed to idols for involvement with it involves worship of dead gods. (*Did.* 6.1–3)

The *Didache* is taking a moderate approach: the covenant, the relationship with God and the demands of a moral life, so that one shared in that covenant, are what is important. On the other details there was freedom to do what one could. This moderation and practical sense has led one commentator to praise this as 'the pastoral genius of the *Didache*' (> Milavec, 1989).

This issue of 'the yoke of the Lord', understood as the details of ritual observance, was one of the major disputes that existed in communities and between churches in the first century. We may think that the *Didache* strikes a sensible middle way, just as later Luke would try to present that same way as the outcome of a harmonious meeting of the apostles in Jerusalem, but it was not anything of the sort. Many held that converts had to be careful observers of the whole law, just as Jewish followers of Jesus had to observe every little 'iota and dot' of the law. However, the solution offered in the *Didache* would become the standard approach as we see when we compare it with Luke's statement in Acts at the very end of the first century or early in the second:

> For it has seemed good to the Holy Spirit and to us to lay upon you no greater burden than these necessary things: that you abstain from what has been sacrificed to idols and from blood and from what is strangled and from unchastity. If you keep yourselves from these, you will do well. Farewell.
>
> (Acts 15.28–29 [RSV])

While Paul, at the same time as the *Didache*, was defending just this approach to the gentile Christians in Corinth who did not even see the need to avoid meat used in sacrifices to the city's gods:

> What do I imply then? That food offered to idols is anything, or that an idol is anything? No, I imply that what pagans sacrifice they offer to demons and not to God. I do not want you to be partners with demons. (1 Cor. 10.19–20 [RSV])

The longer title of the *Didache* is that it is 'the teaching of the Lord to the gentiles' and this little item of wisdom on only asking the gentile converts to do what they are able to do might indicate that this longer title was original, and may even be part of the rationale of the *Didache*.

Clashes of cultures

When we read the *Didache* we are aware of two culture clashes. The first, and obvious one, is that which the early Christians saw between their view of how one should lead a good life and its destiny and that of the Graeco-Roman world around them. The other clash is between how Christians today see their discipleship and the way that discipleship was presented, and understood, in the first century.

The first clash can be seen in the repeated emphasis in the Two Ways on staying away from magic, sorcery, divination and astrology. This might seem like overkill: is it really that serious to go to a fortune-teller? Certainly, since the twelfth century many Christians have consulted astrologers and did not see it as sinful! However, in the Mediterranean world of two millennia ago, to engage in any of these practices was to engage with a whole view of the cosmos that was at odds with a belief in a God who was the creator of all – including angels, demons, stars and the very rocks beneath our feet – and who was also interested in us as people, so interested that he entered a covenant with us. This clash reminds us that the world of the first Christians, despite all our continuities in faith, is not just an earlier version of our world.

The second clash between how we perceive the demands of faith and how they presented them can be seen in attitudes to slavery. We think of slavery as a great crime, an abuse of our fellow human beings that is incompatible with both our common human dignity and our status as children of God. It is interesting to see how with those same assumptions in place, the early Christians saw no problem with slavery. Moreover, we know that this was the standard position among Christians as we see the same view on slavery in Paul's letter to Philemon. Here is how the *Didache* thought that a Christian should treat his slaves (even if they are Christians):

> You shall not give orders to your man-slave or woman-slave when you are angry – remember they hope in the same God as you – because this might cause them to stop respecting God who is over both of you; and remember that he comes to call, without thought of status, those whom the Spirit has prepared.
> And slaves, you should be submissive to your masters with respect and fear as to an image of God.   (*Did.* 4.10–11)

No one today would, I hope, try to present this message as suitable behaviour or advice to give in the name of Christianity. But bear this in mind: until less than 200 years ago most Christians saw nothing essentially wrong with slavery provided one did not abuse one's slaves. This clash of cultures is a reminder that while looking back to the past can remind us of important aspects of Christianity that we have forgotten or undervalued, we must always look back critically. We cannot look back to a 'golden age' or a moment of Christian perfection in an 'age of the saints', nor can we simply seek to hold the past nor any ancient text as having all the answers. Such a backwards vision is both fundamentalist and a denial that perfection only exists at the end of time. Rather, we see the areas where they had insights that we have lost, and are thankful for those insights that we have, but which they lacked.

At this point, it would be a good idea to read the whole of the Two Ways, *Didache* 1–6 (> pp. 161–5), as a single unit: by doing so one gets a sense of its sweep and of how it presents particular commandments and specific sins as flowing from the great commandments and from more general sins. There is a lot more in the text than I have had room to highlight in this chapter.

The next step . . .

We can see the Two Ways as a reworking of the demands of the Deuteronomic covenant from the perspective that the

Anointed One of the Father has come among us. That Anointed One is extending the embrace of that covenant to the nations, and the Two Ways sets out the standard that all, Jew and gentile, must seek if they are to be part of the people of the covenant. But what is the next step along the Path of Life for someone who is accepting the Father's invitation to a relationship and has learned the Way as an apprentice? The next step is to become a member of the Church by being baptized, and the very next words in the *Didache*, after the Two Ways, are: 'With regard to baptism . . .' (*Did.* 7.1). The Spirit was preparing individuals, Jews and Greeks, males and females, slaves and free, and all were to be baptized into one body. This theme laid out implicitly in the *Didache* is one we tend to think of as Paul's view of baptism as set out also in 1 Corinthians 12.13 or Galatians 3.27—4.6; the difference is that Paul is drawing on this practice to make particular theological points, whereas in the *Didache* we find more attention to the practical details of baptism than to its theological explanations.

3

Joining the group

Having started out along the Way of Life, the next step for the person whose call by the Lord had been prepared by the Spirit (*Did.* 4.10) was to join the group, the Church. While the word 'church' conjures up for most people today a negative image of musty buildings, legal structures and clerics, for the early communities the word 'church' (*ekklēsia*) would still have echoed its literal meaning: the 'assembly' of the Lord's people. The word *ekklēsia* was familiar to all Greek-speaking Jews because it was used to translate *qahal* in the Greek version of the Hebrew Scriptures – we render the word with phrases like: 'assembly of the Lord' (Deut. 23.2 [RSV]); 'all the assembly of Israel, men and women' (Josh. 8.35); or 'assembly of God' (Neh. 13.1 [RSV]). 'Church' became our common word because that Greek translation became the basic text of the Scriptures for Christians. But 'being one of the assembly' was not simply a common label: one had to be admitted by one who was already part of the community and a formal ritual of admission set a boundary around the group. This act of being incorporated was called 'baptism'. Here is what the *Didache* has to say about it, and note that the 'you' referred to is in the plural – 'ye' – and the teaching is therefore intended for every member of the group:

> With regard to baptism, here is the teaching:
> You are to baptize in this way.
> Once you have gone back over all that is in the Two Ways, you baptize in the name of the Father and of the Son and of the Holy Spirit in living water.

However, if you do not have access to living water, then baptize in some other water; and if you do not have any cold water, then you can use warm water.

And if you cannot get access to either [running or still water], then pour water three times on the head in the name of the Father and of the Son and of the Holy Spirit.

Moreover, before the baptism takes place, let both the person baptizing and the person who is going to be baptized fast – along with as many others as are able to do so. Indeed, you must instruct the person who is going to be baptized to fast for one or two days before the baptism. (*Did.* 7)

To Christians today this all seems so normal – the actions and the words – that we can easily forget to ask some basic questions. For instance: why did they choose the action of 'being plunged' – the literal meaning of 'being baptized' – as the key event in entering the community; where did the idea of plunging come from; why does joining the community of Jesus need a ritual at all; and how would they have explained the ritual?

The idea of baptism

This might seem a silly question: was not Jesus baptized by John the Baptist (Mark 1.9, followed by Matt. 3.13 and Luke 3.21), did he not engage with his disciples in baptizing (John 4.1–2), and did he not command his followers to make disciples from all the nations and baptize them using the very words we have in the *Didache* (> Matt. 28.19)? However, these Gospel passages, with the possible exception of Mark whose Gospel was being preached before AD 70, are later than the instruction in the *Didache*. Therefore, we have to explain *both* the choice of the action of baptizing *and* how that action was linked with the memory of Jesus in the first churches.

For Jews, the ritual that marked their boundary as a community, and as the assembly who had accepted the covenant, was circumcision. Circumcision, along with the sabbath and the regulations regarding food, was the mark of accepting God's promises (Gen. 17.9–14). By the time of Jesus, indeed for more than a century before his time, circumcision was closely linked to Israel's self-perception as the covenant people of God (1 Macc. 1.14–15, 60–61; 2 Macc. 6.10). It was the most important boundary marker separating Jew from gentile, those within the covenant from those outside it. So there was no need for any other fundamental boundary ritual – a boundary ritual is an action that distinguishes a group from those who are not-belonging-to-the-group, 'the people' as distinct from everyone else.

But there were many other traditions that marked transitions from one state of relationship with God to another for those who were within the covenant community. One such important ritual was that of a bath to cleanse away certain impurities before acts of worship. A leper, for instance, once clear of disease – after seeing a priest – could only be readmitted to the community after washing his clothes, shaving his hair and having had a bath (Lev. 14.2–8). And contacts with 'impure' bodily discharges which could make one unfit to perform the service of God were to be washed away by washing clothes and having a bath (e.g. Lev. 15.2–5). We know from archaeological discoveries that in Jewish towns there were pools for taking these special religious baths, while in Qumran there were numerous pools so that this community could see itself as always pure, and so always ready to offer praise to God. It was this ritual practice that was adopted by John the Baptist to mark out those who had accepted his preaching that the judgement of God was imminent. These were the people who had fled sin and repented, were washed by John in the living, that is, flowing, water of the Jordan, and now purified of sin could withstand coming judgement. John's message was that the crunch was about to come upon a wicked generation: those who listened to him saw the need to separate themselves and be purified of their sins by a bathing. This washing which made his followers into the purified people may have been taken over from existing rites of purification, but it had the effect of making them a group within a group, a people within a people – and, as such, the purification bath became a boundary ritual. The followers of John were a distinct community because each of them had been baptized by him.

In the Gospels, the relationship between John and Jesus is presented, especially in Luke, as one of intimacy, harmony and seamless continuity: they were cousins, John announces Jesus, baptizes him, and then Jesus brings to perfection that which was inaugurated by John the Baptist:

> '"After me comes a man who ranks ahead of me because he was before me." I myself did not know him; but I came baptizing with water for this reason, that he might be revealed to Israel.' And John testified, 'I saw the Spirit descending from heaven like a dove, and it remained on him. I myself did not know him, but the one who sent me to baptize with water said to me, "He on whom you see the Spirit descend and remain is the one who baptizes with the Holy Spirit." And I myself have seen and have testified that this is the Son of God.' (John 1.30–34 [NRSV])

However, this is the picture looking backwards from several generations later, and, more importantly, with hindsight the evangelists saw all that happened as part of God's providential plan. But the relationship was far more fraught. John preached that the judgement of God was coming on a sinful generation – the crunch was coming and only those who set themselves apart would be saved. Jesus seems to have had links with this movement, but broke away from it. His message about the imminent coming of the kingdom was radically different: the Day of the Lord was not a grim day of judgement, but rather the day of the Lord's forgiveness.

In some places in our Gospels (e.g. the image of the sheep and the goats in Matt. 25) there is a sense of dread future judgement, but these instances – which exhibit the more widespread views of the early communities – have to be seen against the broad sweep of Jesus' statements about the coming kingdom where he addresses God as 'Father' and such stories as that about the welcoming father in the parable of the Prodigal Son (Luke 15.11–32), or his own practice in the case of the woman taken in adultery (John 8.2–11) – a story about Jesus whose 'laxity' with regard to judgement shocked many early communities.

His new community was to rejoice that God had shown mercy and that that mercy would extend to all (> Meier, 1994, pp. 116–30). Whether Jesus would have seen any need for a washing to remove the 'impurities' of people before they could see themselves as part of the kingdom is very doubtful. There are so many stories of Jesus and the disciples eating without observing the purity laws (e.g. Mark 7.3), having contact with that which would make them impure, and not worrying about it (Matt. 8.3 and 9.20), and eating with sinners (e.g. Luke 7.34) that it appears that he considered the whole notion of impurity as having been swept away by God's forgiving love. Purity was not a matter of cups and plates, but rather rooting out greed and self-indulgence (> Matt. 23.25). So, even though Jesus had at one stage in his life been baptized, why was there any later use for a notion of the need for a bath for impurity, and why was Jesus remembered as intimately linked with John's bath?

The answer lies in the movement of many of John's followers to become followers of Jesus – and it would seem that with John's death many more of his disciples became followers of Jesus. One might imagine that if someone has left John and followed Jesus, then he or she would simply have jettisoned what was linked with John and adopt what belonged to Jesus! But this is not how human beings act, especially in religious matters: people carry their histories and their precious customs with them into the new situation. Some who changed over to Jesus may have only seen what John and Jesus had in common

such as that the Lord was coming among his people or that
there was another special route distinct from 'ordinary Judaism';
others may have grafted Jesus' teaching into what they had
already heard from John; many others would not have realized
the extent to which John's teaching was still influencing them
even when they thought they had moved from one prophet to
another. The result was that the early communities that looked
to Jesus as the Anointed One actually combined many elements
from John's teaching with elements from that of Jesus. We see
this legacy in Christianity to this day: there are some people
who look to the Gospels and come away with a message of
God's impending judgement, and their outlook is apocalyptic;
others look at the same Gospels and think that this approach
is wrong-headed. The legacy of John's notion of the Day of
the Lord as crunch, while it may not sit well with that of Jesus'
kingdom of welcome, is still with us, and is a theme that
Christians return to from time to time.

One of those elements of John's teaching that was carried
over was the belief that accepting that the kingdom was at hand
formed them into a distinct people apart; they were in a special
relationship to the covenant; and while every Jewish boy was
circumcised, this group was ritually distinct in that everyone
in it, man and woman, had been baptized. For John's followers
this ritual bath was an item of major importance; it was how
they thought of themselves as a group and how others thought
of them – hence the sobriquet given to their prophet: 'the
baptizer' – and as such it was a custom they would have held
as precious. There is a funny phenomenon we see happening
time and again in religion: group practices (the ritual) remain
stubbornly the same, yet how they are explained (the theology)
changes with circumstances. This is counter-intuitive: we might
expect that people would hold onto their theories, and that
practices would vary; but it is almost never like that. A group
that has made the action of 'plunging' a key group moment is
going to keep that custom when they see one leader replaced

by another, and despite the fact that the way they explain the action has changed many times. No doubt when John opted for a bathing he was thinking in terms of the law in Leviticus and of purifying the people before the terrible day of judgement – we see this in references to his preaching 'a baptism of repentance for the forgiveness of sins' (Luke 3.3) – but the practice soon took on the significance of being, for those not in the group, the brand of his followers, while for those in the group it became their badge of identity: we are the community within the larger Israel that is ready for what is coming. Later, when that group came under the influence of Jesus – and now saw themselves as his followers – they continued with this badge of identity. You knew that you were part of this new People of Israel – amidst all the other Jews who were children of the covenant – because you had been through the plunging in the living water (i.e. flowing water). Baptism formed the boundary for John's community, and it migrated to become the boundary for Jesus' community.

However, while the action of baptism seems to have been accepted by all the followers without much difficulty – all groups seem to generate boundary rituals in one way or another – the assimilation of John's teaching with that of Jesus would be no easy matter. In the Gospels we see stories which present the two strands living harmoniously, but the fissures that open up again and again in Christianity – as we shall see later with the practice of fasting – can often be traced to the fact of two very different visions of how God relates to us: one can be traced to John and the other to Jesus. These views were never integrated – that would have been impossible – but were shoved together as if the differences could be passed over. Every so often the glue fails and groups reject either the Jesus or the John vision of God's love. Meanwhile most Christians, for the most part, shuffle on with the 'lumpy mixture' of both that we find in the early churches and their great evangelists. Baptism is a case in point: by the time of John's death it had ceased being simply a requirement of the covenant's law so that people could offer pure service to God and had become a mark of belonging to John's people, then the practice continued and it came to be the mark of belonging to Jesus' people. And as such, it became the key moment of initiation into the Way of Jesus in the *Didache* and has remained a key feature in Christian practice ever since – but even then, the legacy of the 'lumpy mixture' continued in the many divisions that have occurred in the Church over baptism. Some would argue that it was about removing sin that could lead to death (a very John-like view) and so it was very important to baptize infants – and they saw initiation as something happening afterwards; others would see baptism as fundamentally the moment of commitment to Jesus and so would argue that only adults could be baptized. Significantly, in the *Didache* we have the emphasis on the practice, without any attempt at 'explaining' its significance.

Humans are ritual animals

But if baptism came to the followers of Jesus from those who originally followed John the Baptizer, how did it become so important that it is a basic element of the *didache* and the preachers of Jesus? All four of the Gospels have a meeting with John as the crucial moment at the beginning of Jesus' preaching. In Mark, Matthew and Luke there is the scene of John baptizing Jesus (John the Evangelist is nuanced and does not actually say that Jesus was baptized; while the final editor of John's Gospel has Jesus' disciples, but not Jesus himself, baptize). That memory of Jesus being baptized by John had the effect of giving the act of baptism – and, therefore, the custom among John's people – the stamp of approval by Jesus.

But would Jesus have approved of any ritual? There have been groups down the centuries that have assumed either that there was no need for ritual or that ritual was one of the aspects of religion that Jesus abandoned: surely, they argue, his religion was of 'those who worship the Father . . . in spirit and truth' (John 4.24) and had little role for ceremony. Certainly, down the centuries many Christians have taken this line and have thought that all rituals were a distraction; and only continued with baptism and the Eucharist because they were 'explicitly' commanded to do so by the Lord! They were 'the dominical sacraments' and as such were exempt from condemnation (but should be performed with 'as little fuss as possible'). However, rather than starting with theories about what should be the case, let us start with the reality of our human nature.

Imagination makes us human. We understand far more than we see, we know more than we encounter, we learn much besides what we are taught, we communicate far more than we say or write, and what we hear is different from that recorded by tape or transcript. This fact of our nature is both good and bad news for theologians. It is good in so far as it reassures us that human beings cannot be reduced to either isolated centres of rational consciousness or biological processors of sensory stimuli: the world of a human being will always be more than the sum of its parts. It is also good news in that it reminds us that we are ritual animals and liturgy of some sort is 'hard wired' into our existence: we both establish our world and make sense of our living within it through complex social rituals, through community validated narratives, and through symbols that reach us holistically: speaking at once to senses, mind and emotions (> Rothenbuhler, 1998). We in the contemporary Western world may have a strong sense that we can distinguish between 'symbols' and 'reality' – or even have a notion that 'symbols' are opposed to 'reality' – but that belief is most probably just one of the conceits of our particular cultural market place. Being human is being able to read the 'vibes' of a situation or event along with the rationally intended communications of one person to another. Indeed, many would argue that there are human signals that operate within societies at so basic a level of interpersonal communication that we are unconscious of them, or even that such signals are to a large extent beyond our rational control. Thus a gesture that is a fixed part of a formal ritual may equally be a basic gesture that only takes on its most formal aspect when used within that specific ritual: a nod to a passing acquaintance in the street is a ritual action, yet the same notion of acknowledgement can take on a formal ritual form in a salute. Rituals are everywhere in life – not just in musty ceremonies frequented by those who like that sort of thing – because they show us and those around us who we are and what are our most pressing concerns. Our rituals create the world we inhabit and call 'our culture'. So any group who adopt a way of life, link themselves with a particular view of the universe, choose to follow a teacher, or seek to exist with a definite view of themselves and their history – these are the basic forms of all religions – will develop, whether they set out to or not, a set of rituals that give shape to that lifestyle, that commitment, that vision and that world-view.

The early followers of Jesus had all these factors in their background: they had a distinct view of themselves as the people of the mutual relationship (i.e. the covenant) with God; they had a distinctive history; they had their own ritual of worship at the large, group scale in the Temple and at the intimate family level in the Passover and sabbath meals and they had a vision of the universe: one God who was beyond the creation. This relation, vision, history, commitment was even marked on the bodies of their men folk – for they were distinct from the nations surrounding them – by circumcision. Rituals created the people, and it was in the context of those rituals that they told stories and heard preaching. They even had a sacred set of books because the formal recollection of a group's memory and laws always becomes a ritual in itself. Now to any group within that group, all those rituals would simply continue – so, for example, when the early Christians referred to 'the Scriptures' it was those same Scriptures (i.e. what we call 'the Old Testament') they meant; and it would take well over a century for the early stories of the Christians to be ritualized as a sacred memory and gain the cachet of 'Scripture' (i.e. what we call 'the New Testament').

Not only was ritual in the background of those from among the Jewish people who followed John or Jesus, but also those people quickly developed a strong sense of who they were. They were bearing witness to God's initiative; not only had they chosen a life of dedication to the covenant, but also they understood it as the Way of loving service. They thought of themselves as a body; they knew that Jesus had died as a result of this way; and they believed that he was the Lord whom the Father – their new way of addressing God – had raised from the dead. Moreover, they were walking along this Way because the Spirit had called them and enabled them. With such a distinctive view of themselves, the world and God, this new group within the People of Israel would need to evolve rituals that expressed this distinctive identity: this evolution was simply a function of their humanity.

Any group which has:

- a developed sense of belonging – when belonging is more like being a member of a family rather than simply subscribing to a newsletter;
- a firm sense of its own history – a belief about why it came about, what its people have done and what it can do;
- and a clear unifying set of 'facts' – it could be that they all live in the same valley or speak the same language, or it could be, as here, that they all have chosen to live in the same way

will have a very clear sense of its boundaries, and of who is within the group. Furthermore, it will ritualize the gateways in those boundaries so that the whole group have a badge of identity and newcomers know they have crossed a threshold. For the followers of Jesus, that ritual, inherited from John's followers, was baptism.

Accepting Jesus and imagining the community

In Matthew's Gospel, and also in that of Luke, there is a statement of Jesus that must go back to Jesus himself because it contains the implications of the differences between John the Baptist and Jesus – differences that were being ignored by the last quarter of the first century:

> For John came neither eating nor drinking, and they say, 'He has a demon'; the Son of Man came eating and drinking, and they say, 'Look, a glutton and a drunkard, a friend of tax-collectors and sinners!'
>
> (Matt. 11.18–19 [NRSV]/Luke 7.33–34)

Jesus not only proclaimed the closeness of the kingdom of God but also portrayed a loving Father who offered forgiveness and new life. His image of God's call was of outcasts becoming his intimates around his table. And within this environment of welcome, each was to set out on a new path in fulfilling the covenant in love. Those who set out on this path formed a community – and just as Jesus extended his table to prostitutes and tax-collectors, so that community was to be one that was to be characterized by openness. Anyone who wanted to join the Way, and was willing to set out on the Way, could join the Way. It had clear boundaries, but they were looking outwards and the gates on those boundaries had welcome signs to those outside. It is important to note that this is a prominent feature of the Jesus movement – and many who would accept welcome themselves would find offering a similar welcome to those of whom they disapproved far more difficult. Most religious groups are, alas, better at identifying those who should not belong than in offering acceptance – as Paul would point out to the Corinthians in his first letter to them, or (disagreeing with Peter) in his letter to the Galatians over the matter of whether gentile converts had to follow all the law's prescriptions.

The openness that Jesus exemplified and which is seen in the *Didache* – if you accept the Way of life and love then you are ready for baptism without more ado – is quite unusual. Most groups define themselves by who they exclude and so the boundaries have notices like: *only* those who are . . . or have . . . or can do . . . can enter here. The effect of the 'only' is that they tell you this is an *exclusive* group: to understand it, you are to look at who are not allowed to enter, who are excluded. You have to pass the test, and the test is designed to fail all but the select few. In such exclusive communities the aim is to draw the boundaries so that they point out who is outside, and to keep those inside and those outside apart. But the boundary of baptism was an open boundary: any member of the people of God who chose to live the Way could enter, and within a generation it was realized that if the Father's love and forgiveness knew no bounds, then not only those who were already within the covenant but also people everywhere could cross the boundary marked by baptism if they too wanted to enter the community that called God 'Father' and set out on the path of life. Baptism is the ritual that counts you in, and sets a seal on the decision to walk in a certain way. In the first years it was assumed that this new inclusive group lay within the boundaries of the People of Israel marked out by circumcision and so marked-off from the nations.

But within a very short space of time the community whose threshold was baptism was much larger than that of the Jewish covenant – did these new followers of the Way also need to be circumcised and keep the law? This would be a debate that would rumble on for decades, but the significance of baptism as the boundary ritual was steadily growing as the followers of Jesus evolved from being a group within Judaism to being a distinct religion: 'the Christians'. Soon baptism would be the mark of every Christian – and by the time Matthew preached in the 70s or 80s, making disciples, which involved *didache* followed by baptism, from people of every nation was seen as the culmination of Jesus' message (> Matt. 28.19–20). Disciple-ship and baptism was to be open to all, and to embrace men and women, Jews and gentiles, slaves and free. It was to create a boundary that cut across the most ingrained divisions of religion, gender, race and class. However, keeping those divisions at bay within the new religion would be a far more difficult task.

The details of the event

In looking at the oral quality of the *Didache* (> ch. 1) we remarked that becoming a disciple was probably best seen as a process of apprenticeship. A follower of the Way acted as guide and mentor to a person who was seeking to learn how to live the path of Jesus. It would be easy to imagine that a man acted as the teacher for a man, and a woman acted as the teacher for a woman – while much has been made in recent years about how Jesus broke gender boundaries, we should not imagine that his followers found this easy. Paul, for example, is clear that baptism, being in Christ, cuts across the gender divide ('there is no longer male and female; for all of you are one in Christ Jesus' – Gal. 3.28), but Paul's followers around the end of the first century who wrote in his name the letter we call '1 Timothy' were far more troubled by the notion of a woman being engaged in teaching (*didaskein*) a man: 'I permit no woman to teach or to have authority over a man' (1 Tim. 2.12 [NRSV]). This may have been simply making custom into a regulation: men can act as guides in transmitting the *didache* to men and women, but women can only guide women. But a common point seems to be: whoever taught the apprentice disciple the Way was the one who finally admitted him/her to the community by baptizing the person. This is shown in that the instruction 'you baptize in this way' is given in the plural (literally: 'ye baptize') and it is addressed to the whole com-munity. There is no hint that there was a special designated person who baptized or that the baptizer had a special role – and there were people with special roles (> ch. 6) in the community. The task of forming new disciples, of training apprentice followers of Jesus' Way fell on all in the church, and so all could bring their pupils to the point when they would introduce them to the church by baptizing them. This might seem strange as rarely today, in most churches, are people baptized by anyone other than a 'minister'. However, the memory of the earlier practice is still remembered. Even churches with a very structured view of ministry (e.g. Catholicism) still hold that anyone can baptize – indeed must do so in case of need – while seeing such baptisms as 'extra ordinary'.

John's baptism was given in a river out in the wilderness – note it is in raw nature that his baptism was given and not in a special ritual bath – and the notion of being in the wilderness, away from human works, was intended no doubt to instil the notion that his baptism was a return to the time of Israel in the desert during the exodus from Egypt and a new crossing of the Jordan to become renewed dwellers in the Land of the Covenant. The desert and the Jordan were full of memories for those to whom he preached. This memory of river remained with his followers even after they moved over to Jesus. The evangelist John recalls, much later than the *Didache*, that 'John [the Baptist] also was baptizing at Aenon near Salim because water was abundant there; and people kept coming and were being baptized' (John 3.23 [NRSV]). And this choice of a river was seen as the ideal location for a baptism by the early churches: this is indicated by the use of the term 'living water' which means the flowing water of a river as distinct from the still water that is stored in cisterns or found in wells. Indeed, this memory and preference is confirmed by the use of 'living water' as a metaphor in the preaching (*kerugma*): standing by the well Jesus promises the Samaritan woman 'living water' (John 4.10–11) and also John the evangelist compares the Spirit in the believers' hearts to 'a river of living water' (John 7.38–39).

For the communities a baptism in a river was pregnant with memories: of the desert, of crossing the Red Sea and the Jordan, of John baptizing, of Jesus being baptized. And it was gaining new memories of being the place of the new life of the Spirit, given by Jesus, within their hearts.

But not every community could get access to a river, so just as there was a practical compromise on observing the law of Moses such that gentile converts were asked only to do as much as they were able (*Did.* 6.2), now they can use any other water (i.e. water from a cistern or well) if they cannot get to a river. Wherever the community was located, there it could baptize: there was no specific sacred place to which they had to track off. Moreover, if you cannot get baptized in cold water, then it is all right to use warm water! Much ink has been spilled over why this detail has been added here, but I believe the answer is simple. While the idea of a cold bath might not trouble some, for others it would be a worry and such worries would distract the apprentice from the Way: so they simply agreed that s/he could be baptized in a warm water pool such as were to be found in many of the wealthier houses of the Roman world. The more important point is this: baptism was important as marking the completion of apprenticeship and the entry to the community, but they were not to get too worked up about the ritual details. Baptism was not a magical rite, unlike other initiation ceremonies into religious movements in the Graeco-Roman world, where if any little detail were left out then the candidate would not be 'really done'. This sense of practicality, and not paying too much attention to material details, reaches its highpoint when the *Didache* says that if you cannot find a place to have a full plunging then simply baptize by pouring water three times on the head. Ritual was a boundary marker, not a process where every detail was a matter of life and death. Down the centuries many Christians have become so obsessed with the details of ritual – thinking of it in a manner akin to how we view correct surgical procedures today: one slip and it could cost a patient's life – that they have made those details the cause of divisions among Christians and within churches! We still have much to learn from the *Didache* with its insistence on setting out on the way of love, alongside a balanced practicality about ritual forms.

Last, there is the instruction to fast before the baptism. The *Didache* sees this as very important for the candidate – it repeats its message to stress the point – and it desires that it involve as many as possible in the community the candidate is about to enter. And again we see the *Didache* setting out the ideal, but also being pragmatic. Get as many as possible to fast, at least the baptizer and the candidate, but at the very least the candidate for two days, or, if even that is too difficult, then just one day! But why fast if baptism is the culmination of a process of entering the group? How could fasting assist the process?

We see fasting as something punitive or restorative. Either fasting is penitential – the notion of taking on suffering to somehow 'make up' for past sins; or fasting is restorative in the sense that we have over-indulged, and now by depriving ourselves we are training ourselves in proper discipline. But there is another strand to fasting in Judaism that we have all but forgotten: fasting as preparing and fine-tuning ourselves so that we can appreciate an encounter with God (> ch. 4). This could be described as fasting as 'psyching-ourselves-up' for the significant moment of baptism. When Jews in Jesus' time recalled Moses receiving the law on Sinai they remembered that he had to prepare for this meeting by fasting for 40 days (Exod. 34.28). Likewise, Daniel fasted while he awaited his revelation (Dan. 10.3). The communities of the Jesus movement would also have thought of him fasting as a preparation for the start of his public ministry (> Mark 1.13/Matt. 4.2/Luke 4.2). So by fasting the candidate was being finally prepared for formally setting out on the Way – but this was a path she or he would follow in company, and so the whole community by fasting was helping the candidate with her/his preparation for this moment of change in her/his life (> O'Loughlin, 2003a, pp. 95–100).

Knowing what the *Didache* tells us about fasting before the event of baptism, we are then able to understand other references to fasting from the early Church. When Luke describes how Paul was baptized – a description that is later than the *Didache* – we see that he believes that Paul followed what was clearly the standard practice and routine of the churches. For the three days between the revelation on the Damascus road and his baptism, Paul neither ate nor drank (Acts 9.9–18). Likewise, before Paul set aside Barnabas and Saul for special work, Luke points out that they prayed and fasted (Acts 13.1–2); and when Paul was about to entrust the care of a church to elders he did so with prayer and fasting (Acts 14.23). Incidentally, this practice of fasting before baptism continued for many centuries – we have many references to it in second-century documents – and it is the origin of the season of fasting before Easter, called 'Lent' in English. Easter Night was the great moment for baptisms and it was prepared for by a fast of 40 days by the whole community. Later, when infant baptisms became the norm (and these did not take place at the Easter Vigil) the custom of the Lenten fast continued – and acquired a new explanation as a time of penance.

Initiation

What is important in baptism is not the details of the ritual but that it marks a moment of decision in life: now, fully trained and shaped as a disciple, someone sets out in a new direction on life's journey. Baptism is a moment in a process: the preparation by the Spirit, then the apprenticeship with the teacher, then life moving forward as part of the community of disciples. We sometimes think that baptism took place immediately someone had recognized the power of the gospel. We then point to the story of Philip baptizing the Ethiopian eunuch after he had explained how the Scriptures were fulfilled in Jesus (Acts 8.26–40) or how Paul baptized the jailer in Thyatira, along with his whole family one night 'without delay' (Acts 16.25–34). However, the whole point about these stories is that they are the exceptional cases – and so worthy of dramatic note which show that the normal practice was otherwise. Discipleship had to be learned: it was not the passing whim of a moment. A period of learning with one member of the community as teacher, then a time of fasting, and then baptism marking the beginning of the new Path of Life.

Explanations

Rituals are events in themselves. Normally we do not ask why we shake hands, bring flowers, or join our hands in prayer: we just do it. But when someone does not know our rituals we are faced with the question of why do we do this or that, or we ask what the ritual means. Then follows an explanation in which we either tell how we imagine the ritual originated or else try to explain what it means now by 'reading' the various elements of the ritual as if it were an allegorically rich play. Most Christians today would be able to give several of these explanations of baptism. Here is an example: why do we do it? Because Jesus' last command to us was to do it, and he is Lord, so we do it! Or this one: water washes us and makes us clean, so pouring water over us in baptism washes away sins or 'symbolizes' them being washed away! Or, water that covers us would drown us, so this is passage from death to the old self and a birth as a new self. Or we might explain it by pointing to the font/pool as the birthing pool of Christians. There are umpteen such explanations and most of them can be tracked back to the first century and the writings of Paul (e.g. Rom. 6.4) and the evangelist John (John 3.3–6). The strange thing about all such explanations is that while each seems to 'make sense' of the ritual, they are all different and they do not dovetail together despite the desperate efforts of many fundamentalists!

The actual custom of the community is the fact, the new life is the reality, and the 'explanations' are always secondary. The custom forms the continuity, the explanations change. We should think of the ritual as a great drama where every person who attends a performance can take away a new meaning from it. The drama is the thing, and the many interpretations are a tribute to its depth and richness.

This is an important point to remember when we read the *Didache*. The *Didache* tells the details of the custom – something each disciple needs to know so that she/he can initiate another – but it does not give us any 'explanation'. That is something that the teacher can draw out in response to questions, or they can take it from one of the many 'explanations' that were being preached among the communities. Baptism as with all other Christian liturgy is an event – which can indeed generate any number of explanations/theologies; but it is neither a theology class nor some abstract chunk of doctrine being simplified by role-play.

4

Prayer and fasting

The figure of Judith – one of the heroines who saved her people – is not one with which we are very familiar; indeed, some churches no longer even print the book of Judith in their Bibles. But the story was very popular around the time of Jesus, and part of its popularity was derived from the fact that it is a very good story. While the storyline is religious – how good Jews should behave – it tells the story with all the elements of a thriller movie with a woman in the lead role. Looking at Judith in the story (the plot is set in the sixth century BC, but the story was written sometime between 150 and 100 BC), we see the ideal of religious behaviour regarding fasting and prayer that would have been deep inside the religious culture of those who first followed Jesus. The story is set just after the exile and King Nebuchadnezzar – a proverbial bad-guy – has sent an army led by Holofernes – another bad-guy – to destroy the people and carry away all that they have. Faced with this calamity, the High Priest in Jerusalem orders prayer and fasting:

> So the Israelites did as they had been ordered by the high priest Joakim and the senate of the whole people of Israel, in session at Jerusalem. And every man of Israel cried out to God with great fervour, and they humbled themselves with much fasting.
>
> (Judith 4.8–9 [NRSV])

Meanwhile, in the enemy camp Holofernes is told that, so long as Israel serves God, God will defend them – this is the basic covenant – and so if he marches against them, he will fail (Judith 5.20–21). But this does not scare him and he sets off with a massive army confident that Israel 'will not be able to resist our mighty cavalry' (Judith 6.3). Holofernes then decides that he will lay siege to the first of their towns, 'Bethulia' (a fictional place chosen so that no town could claim Judith as one of its own, and thereby distract any attention from Jerusalem), and drive its inhabitants to surrender through hunger and thirst. Eventually, the people decide they have had enough and say they want to give in: God has abandoned them and is punishing their sins (Judith 7.1–28). Uzziah their leader asks them to hold on for just five days more, because 'by that time the Lord our God will turn his mercy to us again, for he will not forsake us utterly' (Judith 7.30). Then enters Judith.

Judith was both rich and beautiful (the story gives many details about her clothes and jewellery); all spoke well of her and knew she 'feared God with great devotion' (Judith 8.8). Three years and four months earlier she had been widowed and from the death of her husband Manasseh she had dressed as a widow; she spent her nights in prayer; and 'she fasted all the days of her widowhood, except the day before the sabbath and the sabbath itself, the day before the new moon and the day of the new moon, and the festivals and days of rejoicing of the house of Israel' (8.6 [RSV]). When she heard what Uzziah had said she was furious: she saw it as putting God to the test with an ultimatum – save us in five days or we will give in! She then gives out a key piece of teaching about prayer:

Do not try to bind the purposes of the Lord our God; for God is not like a human being, to be threatened, or like a mere mortal, to be won over by pleading. Therefore, while we wait for his deliverance, let us call upon him to help us, and he will hear our voice, if it pleases him.   (Judith 8.16–17 [NRSV])

She then tells the people that God will deliver Israel through her hand: she will be the saviour sent by God (Judith 8.33). To prepare for her task she begins to pray at 'the very moment when the evening incense was being offered in Jerusalem' (Judith 9.1) and pleads that God will hear her tears. Then she dresses up 'to entice the eyes of all the men who might see her' (Judith 10.4 [RSV]), leaves the city, and is apprehended by an enemy patrol. Asked who she is she says that she is fleeing the Hebrews and wants to see Holofernes and give him information about his enemies. Amazed by her beauty, the patrol brings Judith into his tent and she declares that she will tell him when the people have sinned and therefore the right time to attack. Over the next three days she prays, avoids unclean food, and purifies herself by bathing each day (Judith 12.7). Finally, Holofernes decides to seduce her; she accepts his advances and drinks with him until he is drunk; then they go to bed and he sleeps. Then, praying for strength, Judith decapitates him, places his head in a bag, and with her maid – on the pretence of going out to pray – makes her getaway. You can guess the outcome: when the Israelites see the head they rejoice and praise God; when Holofernes' army see the head on Bethulia's walls they despair. Israel is triumphant, Judith sings a great thanksgiving song in Jerusalem (Judith 16.1–17), and they all live in security and peace (> Moore, 1985).

But what has this ancient thriller to do with the *Didache*? If you want to understand modern culture, then it is a good idea to see the sort of stories we find attractive on television; so to understand an earlier culture, it is very valuable to see the sort of stories that attracted them. The story of Judith was popular (> Maher, 2003), so note the themes of covenant, God sending a saviour, the notion of fasting linked with prayer, and the notion of fasting and praying at specific times which united prayers in scattered places with the sacrifice in the Temple in Jerusalem. Indeed, we could look at the Judith story as a guide to the spirituality of the sort of family in which Jesus grew up, and of the families whose sons and daughters would become his followers and the first users of the *Didache*.

Now let us read what the *Didache* says about fasting and prayer:

> You must not let your days of fasting be at the same time as those of the hypocrites. They fast on the second day of the sabbath [i.e. Monday] and on the fifth day of the sabbath [i.e. Thursday], so you should hold your fasts on the fourth day of the sabbath [i.e. Wednesdays] and on the Day of Preparation [i.e. Fridays].
> Nor should you offer prayers as the hypocrites do.
> Rather, you should pray like this, just as the Lord commanded in his gospel:
>> Our Father, who is in the heaven
>> Hallowed be your name
>> Your kingdom come
>> Your will be done on earth as it is in heaven
>> Give us this day our daily bread
>> And forgive us our debt as we forgive our debtors
>> And do not lead us in the trial
>> But deliver us from evil
>> For yours is the power and glory for ever.
> Say this prayer three times each day. (*Did.* 8.1–3)

As with the information on baptism, this might all seem straightforward. The Lord's Prayer in this form – let us ignore for a moment the slight change at the end of the prayer – is the prayer of all Christians everywhere. And for many Christians fasting, on specific days, is, or was until recent times, a normal part of their religious lives. Even the statements about not fasting nor praying 'as the hypocrites do' are familiar: similar statements can be found in Matthew's Gospel at 6.5 and 15. Still today, in a secular culture, we know about Mardi Gras, the Carnival and Pancake Tuesday: all reminders of when whole communities fasted. Fish still appears on menus on Friday: a recollection of when Catholics fasted from meat. We are also familiar with similar instructions in other religions: Muslims pray five times each day at specific times and they fast in

Ramadan. So what is significant about these instructions apart from their quaintness?

Fasting

When we look at the Jewish writings from before the time of Jesus (e.g. the book of Judith) and at early Christian books (e.g. the *Didache* and Matthew's Gospel) we learn that fasting was seen as intrinsically linked to personal prayer – these were twin columns in the spirituality of the pious member of the community. And with prayer and fasting often went a third element: almsgiving (e.g. *Did.* 1.6; and Matt. 6.2–4). We see the three linked in the story of the Pharisee praying who points out that he fasts twice a week and gives tithes of all he gets (Luke 18.11–12). Prayer without fasting seemed to lack serious-ness: words seem such fluffy things! But when you feel some-thing in your stomach, then you are in earnest with your words. Then you are taking prayer seriously and asking God to take your needs seriously.

Moreover, as we saw in the last chapter, once a religious practice has become a regular custom, then it becomes ingrained in our lives and imaginations and it will persist come what may! So the practices of Israel remained with the new group within Israel (the followers of Jesus); and then, later, when the parting of the communities into separate religions came about, the followers of Jesus continued the practices. Fasting linked with prayer in the churches is therefore another part of the legacy of Judaism. However, the reality was not nearly so smooth. We can set the teaching on fasting within a context of disagreements between the approaches of normal Jewish practice (including that of John the Baptist) on the one hand and that of Jesus on the other. We can also locate what became standard Christian teaching on fasting within a dispute between 'ordinary Jews' and 'Jews who are followers of Jesus' about fast-ing and their sense of common identity – an early indication of how the communities were pulling apart even before AD 70, from which time we see the groups go more and more their own ways while each side sought to place clear distance between itself and the other.

One of the features of Jesus' behaviour that shocked many religious people at the time was his indifference to all the customs relating to food: what to eat and not eat, when not to eat, and with whom not to eat. Not only did this put him at odds with the 'officials' of Judaism but also it made him clearly different from John the Baptist. Jesus was prepared to liken life with the Father to a banquet with an open welcome (Luke 14), and this was anticipated in his own joy and openness in dining – there was little attention to fasting. We see this in the statement:

> For John the Baptist has come eating no bread and drinking no wine; and you say, 'He has a demon.' The Son of man has come eating and drinking; and you say, 'Behold, a glutton and a drunkard, a friend of tax collectors and sinners!'
> (Luke 7.33–34 [RSV]/Matt. 11.18–19)

which we can trust as a historical memory because it is so much at variance with the fasting practices of the churches where these Gospels were preached. We also see this divergence of Jesus from the customs of fasting in Mark 2.18–20 [RSV]:

> Now John's disciples and the Pharisees were fasting; and people came and said to him, 'Why do John's disciples and the disciples of the Pharisees fast, but your disciples do not fast?' And Jesus said to them, 'Can the wedding guests fast while the bridegroom is with them? As long as they have the bridegroom with them, they cannot fast. The days will come, when the bridegroom is taken away from them, and then they will fast in that day.'

The implication here is that so long as Jesus was with them, they need not fast: but when he would not be with them, then they could fast! So, was fasting to begin on the day of Ascension? Not quite! Because for the evangelists the risen Lord is with his disciples at all times, and the only time that the Lord was not with them was during his three days 'in hell' between the crucifixion and Easter morning. This reading of Mark (and the other evangelists: Matt. 9.14–17; and Luke 5.33–39) is confirmed by a resurrection story that has survived from *The Gospel according to the Hebrews*. There we hear about James, Jesus' brother, who has fasted from the time of the crucifixion and then meets the risen Jesus who tells James that he can end his fast, and the breakfast takes place with Jesus sharing a eucharistic meal with him (> O'Loughlin, 2009). For some, the sadness implicit in fasting was incompatible with the Father's all-embracing love and the continual presence of Jesus in the midst of his disciples. But just as John's disciples brought baptism and the notion of the impending crunch of God's justice, so too they brought his earnestness about fasting, and for many more fasting was so embedded in their notions of living an orderly devout life that the idea that Jesus would be 'against it' seemed too much! So while it was fine for Jesus himself not to fast, or for the disciples who were with him in Galilee, for them, in communities more than a decade later, fasting was the norm. The solidity of established custom in piety was far more powerful than the seemingly insubstantial image of God that Jesus proclaimed. His disciples might refer to God as 'Father' but for many of them – including many trained in the harder vision of John the Baptist – God was still a fearsome Justice who was more likely to hear those prayers backed by fasting. But for the young apprentices learning the *didache*, all such subtleties belonged elsewhere: they would fast and pray with the community.

But there is another tension regarding fasting just below the surface of the *Didache*. One of the indicators of the early date of the *Didache* is the easy familiarity it assumes with the patterns of Jewish life in the generation before AD 70. While the *Didache* assumes that gentiles are being brought into the community – and not necessarily being circumcised – it is also clear that most of the community think of themselves and their lives within the customs and framework of a Jewish community. We see this not only in that the community is sticking with the Jewish practice of twice-weekly fasts but that also they are still naming the days of the week using the Jewish system of reckoning. For Jews at the time the week ended with the day of rest, the sabbath; but the days of the following week were identified by being counted after that sabbath. The seven-day week was already a feature of Graeco-Roman life at this time, but in Greek and Roman society the days were distinguished by names linking each day to a planet (both the Sun and the Moon were planets in their eyes because they wandered across a belt – the zodiac – of the fixed stars; see Table 4.1).

Table 4.1 Days of the week

Jewish name	Gentile name	Our name
First day of the week	Day of the Sun	Sunday
Second day of the week	Day of the Moon	Monday
Third day of the week	Day of Mars	Tuesday
Fourth day of the week	Day of Mercury	Wednesday
Fifth day of the week	Day of Jupiter	Thursday
Preparation Day	Day of Venus	Friday
Sabbath	Day of Saturn	Saturday

The *Didache* makes clear that others with whom its readers are in religious contact – and with whom there is friction as we see in the reference to them as 'hypocrites' – fast on Mondays and Thursdays: so they will do otherwise. It is a sad phenomenon of human history that any two religious groups which are very close in beliefs tend to blacken each other's image by declaring them 'traitors', 'hypocrites' or only a sham of the real thing: and we see a case here. The sadder aspect here is that it was because both parties shared a common origin in the covenant – and so have common views of fasting and prayer – that the one group was deliberately seeking to set its times of fasting in such a way that it was not in union with the others. So when most Jews were fasting on Mondays and Thursdays (note what we saw in the Judith story: she fasted every day except Fridays and Saturdays), the disciples of Jesus would fast on Wednesdays and Fridays, the second choice indicating that, although they still used the Jewish way of reckoning time, the sabbath (a key marker of Jewish identity) was already receding from their consciousness (otherwise they would not have fasted on the Day of Preparation). We shall see more about this move to 'the Lord's Day' (i.e. Sunday) in the next chapter.

Many people reading this – and many who have written on the *Didache* indeed – have found this move of the days on which people should fast very perplexing: how does it make one different from someone else to simply make a choice of a different day? This incomprehension arises from our modern approach to time as a commodity. We live in a world of 'time' and 'time off'; put another way, 'time' is regular work and then when we are 'not doing something productive' (i.e. working/ producing) then we can do what we like (e.g. in the evenings and at the weekend), and anything that belongs to religion automatically belongs in this section. So, today if anyone fasts, it is taken for granted that this must not interfere with the work; it is a private matter for her/him. However, this attitude to time is recent in our society (> Thompson, 1967). In earlier societies, time is the common commodity which unites the whole group, and in which the individual has to make time for that which is not belonging to the group. Think of how the call from the minaret can mark time in an Arab city or how the bell regulates time in a monastery: time, sharing time, unites all those who share it. Today, we only get odd glimpses of this way of thinking as when we want to be with friends for a wedding and say, 'I just could not miss this!' – but, for most of

us, time is what we see on our watches, not what our neighbours
are doing at the same time. To share a time is to be united with
people: to fast *deliberately* at a different time is to separate from
others. We see this notion of shared time in many ways in
the time of Jesus. In the Judith story, she was careful to make
her prayer *at the same time* as the offering in Jerusalem: by
sharing the same time, her prayer was united with that of the
High Priest in the Temple. She was not just one person praying
alone, she was praying with Israel as a single corporate person
(Judith 9.1). In the Dead Sea Scrolls we see the opposite attitude
towards Jerusalem: some Jews believed that the Jerusalem priesthood was corrupt, and a sign of their corruption was that they
fasted, and performed other religious acts, following the 'wrong
calendar' – so the people in Qumran down by the Dead Sea
believed that they kept themselves pure by making sure their
festivals did not coincide with those in Jerusalem (> Vermes,
1962, pp. 42–4). This attitude to time can also be seen in the
Gospel of John. In his timing of the death of Jesus (different
to Mark, Matthew and Luke) the crucifixion takes place at
the same time *before* the Passover that the lambs were being
slaughtered in the Temple: his message, often lost on us, is that
'the Lamb of God, who takes away the sin of the world' (John
1.29 [RSV]), by being put to death *at the same time*, is replacing
the other sacrifice.

By fasting together on fixed days, the community of the
Didache is fasting as a group: it is *the group* who prays. They
are forming a single body at prayer, and so as a 'new Israel' this
single prayer is heard. The fasting regulations are, therefore,
not to be understood as simply a matter of convenience, rules
set out for good order in the community. It is important to
have agreed days so that they can all fast together, and therefore
the prayer of their fasting be heard as one prayer from one
people. Moreover, while they as Jesus' disciples wanted to pray
as one, they no longer wanted to be united with the prayer of
those Jews who were not following Jesus. The split between the

groups that ended up evolving into two distinct religions was already present on the horizon.

It is also worth thinking about some of the practical strife this break in the pattern of fasting would have caused in the case of a single household where some became followers of Jesus and fasted on Wednesdays and Fridays, while others did not. We have no evidence that allows us to glimpse such a situation, but it may be one of the reasons why we hear of 'households' being baptized (e.g. Acts 16.34 and 18.8) while we hear the community being described as the 'household of God' (e.g. Eph. 2.19; and 1 Pet. 4.17). In effect, if one member of a household became a Christian, it affected everyone she/he lived with: such a situation might help us make sense of the strange prophecy about domestic turmoil we find in Matthew (10.34–39) and Luke's (12.49–53, 14.26–27) preaching.

The 'Our Father'

We said in Chapter 1 that there is good reason to believe that the *Didache* was learned off by heart so that every disciple could both know the basic ways of living and practising as a follower of Jesus and also be able to initiate new converts. But there is only one part that is still committed to memory by modern Christians: the Lord's Prayer. It is one of the few elements in Christians' worship today where one can get widespread agreement (more or less) about what to do or say: at the suggestion that a group recite the Lord's Prayer, most will both agree to the suggestion and be able to say it. Ask them why it is the common prayer, however, and not only will certain modern divisions between them appear but also some interesting bits of confusion about its origins.

So why is the 'Our Father' still important? For some, it is because it is given by Jesus in the Bible – because it is in 'the Bible' it is acceptable and authentic. For others, it is because it is in the tradition of prayer by the community ever since the time of Jesus – and as such it was witnessed in the Gospels – that it is sacred. So we have to ask a basic question: did Jesus come to form a community (which then might use books such as our Gospels) or did he come to convey a body of information (the Gospels) and the community was the collection of those who accepted that information? For the historian, the second option is clearly ridiculous: Jesus is almost alone among religious leaders in not writing a book; all his work was focused on establishing a community of disciples, the ingathering of Israel that was the 'kingdom'; and the books only came along afterwards as a consequence of trying to preserve memories intact within that community. So how did the community get this prayer?

Most people combine some of Matthew's preaching with some of Luke's preaching – stories that were not intended to be harmonized – to produce this: one day the disciples asked Jesus to teach them how to pray and he taught them the prayer we now use: *Our Father, who art in heaven* . . . A first step is to unravel this confusion, and then look at the *Didache*.

Step 1

In Luke 11.1–4 (rsv) we have a story that not only puts the prayer onto the lips of Jesus but also actually has him give it to his followers as an answer to their desire to be taught to pray:

> He was praying in a certain place, and when he ceased, one of his disciples said to him, 'Lord, teach us to pray, as John taught his disciples.' And he said to them, 'When you pray, say:
> Father, hallowed be thy name. Thy kingdom come. Give us each day our daily bread; and forgive us our sins, for we ourselves forgive every one who is indebted to us; and lead us not into temptation.'

But the point to note is that this is not the prayer we say; but this is the scene we remember as the prayer's 'origin'.

Step 2

In Matthew (6.9–13), in the middle of the Sermon on the Mount, which has spoken about genuine fasting, almsgiving and prayer, we have this:

> Pray then like this: Our Father who art in *the heavens*,
> Hallowed be thy name.
> Thy kingdom come.
> Thy will be done, on earth as it is in heaven.
> Give us this day our daily bread;
> And forgive us our debts, as we also have forgiven our debtors;
> And lead us not into temptation, but deliver us from evil.

And some of the manuscripts add: 'For thine is the kingdom and the power and glory for ever. Amen', at the end of the prayer.

This last phrase was not part of the original of Matthew's Gospel because his next verse, 6.14, is a comment elaborating 6.12: 'And forgive us our debts, as we also have forgiven our debtors' (NRSV). But we should note two points here. First, Matthew does not say 'who art in heaven' but 'who art in the heavens'. Second, although the phrase 'for thine is the kingdom . . .' was not part of Matthew's original text, that does not mean it was not part of the original prayer (remember that the prayer was being recited long before Matthew preached his Gospel, and when he included it in this great Sermon he assumed that all his audience already knew it. But note, as with Luke, the prayer as it is found in Matthew is *not* the prayer we recite, although it is very like it.

Step 3

Our prayer is only known in Greek, and the phraseology of the prayer in Greek is beautifully balanced in its language. It has been smoothed out in such a way that it is easy to remember because there is a certain rhythm to it and so it trips off the tongue easily (> Henderson, 1992). This shows that between the time that Jesus introduced the new way of addressing God as 'father', along with his new way of expressing the covenant, 'forgive us as we forgive', and the time of the communities which used the *Didache*, the prayer had evolved in the usage of the disciples to produce in Greek a form that is ideal for recitation, and indeed for saying in a group (in any text recited by a group, if the phrases do not end smoothly, then the common recitation will become noise: and that does not happen to our prayer in Greek).

Step 4

In the *Didache* we have the prayer as it is recited, but with a small variation in the last phrase: the word 'kingdom' is omitted, and there is no 'original' context: just pray as 'the Lord commanded in his gospel'.

We can assemble these pieces so that they both all hang together and throw further light on the life of the early churches. The notion that Jesus wanted his followers to address God in a manner similar to what we say is common to all: indeed, the *Didache* is the most explicit. His prayer evolved among Greek-speaking disciples into the prayer we know: a prayer that began with 'Our Father' and ended with 'and the glory. Amen'. This was committed to memory as a central plank of discipleship. As such it became part of the *didache* and hence its place here in our *Didache*. But why has one of the final words been missed out in the text as we have it? The last words of the prayer are unstable in several ancient translations, not just here. Because this prayer was so valued it was described as part of the 'gospel' (as the *Didache* says) and so preachers of the gospel included it in their Gospels (hence it is in both Matthew and Luke). Matthew took the standard wording of the prayer and incorporated it into a whole sermon on Christian spirituality. Luke saw it was part of the training of disciples and so located it after a request from the disciples that their teacher teach them to pray. Luke either knew a form of the prayer that dated from before the balanced version came into general use, or else he recognized that the prayer as it was being recited was in an evolved state and so made it look more 'primitive' in his preaching so as to make his audience think about what they were reciting by heart. Whereas in the *Didache* we have a text that has the recited form of the community, but at a point before the final phrase has its final form: to the Father belonged the power and the glory.

Key points

While everyone reading the *Didache* wonders about the variations between the prayer there and the form of the prayer in Matthew's Gospel, all those details should not obscure the two key points about the prayer that the *Didache* brings before us.

First, the use of a short, formal prayer, said regularly, was held by all disciples to be a commandment of the Lord. As such it was a central aspect of their discipleship. Our first-century texts link it to being part of the path of discipleship, and link it with other aspects of discipleship such as fasting and alms. It was to be learned by heart and was to shape the disciples in the ways that they prayed. When any two Christians met, here was a prayer they could together make to the Father.

Second, while we are often struck by its use of 'Father' and the way it makes intercession and recalls the covenant – all of which point to it being the equivalent of the prayer offered in the Temple in Jerusalem – we often fail to note that it is written in the plural from our side. The prayer is to *our* Father . . . give *us* this day *our* daily bread . . . forgive *us* *our* trespasses as *we* forgive . . . against *us* and lead *us* . . . but deliver *us* . . . Amen. This was not the prayer of the individual but of the community (> Rordorf, 1980–2). Even when an individual recites it, she/he does so in union with the community into which she/he was baptized, and with whom he/she gathers to eat, and with whom he/she travels the road of life. The community as a whole offered the Temple's sacrifice through the High Priest: now, this is also the prayer of the whole people. We saw this emphasis on joining an individual's prayer virtually with that of the whole community in the story of Judith; now, by using the plural, this prayer meant that the individual was not to see herself/himself praying alone, but always, at least virtually, as part of the whole.

Three times daily

By the time of Jesus there were many groups within Judaism that considered regular prayer – quite apart from the formal liturgy of the Temple in Jerusalem – to be the mark of a good and true child of the covenant. So Daniel, that paragon of the faithful Jew, is presented as going 'to his house where he had windows in his upper chamber open toward Jerusalem; and he got down upon his knees three times a day and prayed and gave thanks before his God' (Dan. 6.10). But at what hour were these three times? Neither the book of Daniel (completed in the second century BC) nor the *Didache* says what those times were. But a moment's thought suggests that anything that is done three times a day would point to doing it morning, noon and evening. Such a set of times are easy to establish in a culture without clocks, and we find support for this idea in Psalm 55.17, another work known as *2 Enoch* 51.4, and some of the documents found in Qumran (> Bradshaw, 1979). So here is another religious practice with which the whole community was familiar and found easy to follow, and which was now given a new dimension by having the prayer of Jesus used at those times.

But why repeat a prayer three times every day? First, it is important to note that this is a modern question: most religions are deeply committed to patterns of time when prayers and rituals are repeated forming, as it were, the background 'mood music' to all that the people do. In many religions there is a pattern of repetition in each of time's cycles: the day, the week, the month and the year. Hence, a repetition of our basic prayer morning, noon and evening, in time's shortest natural cycle, the day, may answer a basic human need to acknowledge God (even if this is a need we do not feel within our industrialized time). Second, there is another aspect to Jewish prayer which became a central aspect of Christian prayer. The prophets looked forward to a time when Israel would offer a pure sacrifice in all places (> Mal. 1.11, quoted in *Did.* 14.3), and there would be a time when God would be offered mercy and steadfast love and not sacrifice (> Hos. 6.6; and Matt. 9.13 and 12.7). At the core of this vision was that of a holy, pure people offering prayer without ceasing: all the people would behave as if they were priests. This is, indeed, the standard by which the Pharisees sought to live. Jesus takes over this notion and his community of disciples are seen as a priestly people, who can call on God – as the Levitical priests did – and even call him 'Father'. When this community prayed together it was offering its sacrifice as a priestly people. And with their communal prayer, recited as a group (physical or virtual) every day – at the beginning, middle and end – wherever they were, they were praying that the kingdom would grow, and were that new kingdom in their action.

Liturgical time

Jesus was born within a pious Jewish family in a liturgy-rich environment – and the legacy of those surroundings can still be found, if sometimes in an obscured way, in Christian liturgy. There was the liturgy of the Jerusalem Temple with its great feasts (Jesus took part: Luke 2.41), there was the weekly synagogue liturgy (Jesus took part: Luke 4.16), and there were the domestic liturgies of the sabbath and other meals, daily prayers and days of fasting. This all took place within a cycle of feasts: such as Tabernacles, Atonement, Pentecost and the Passover. We know that this pattern formed the community around Jesus and that the first communities after the resurrection adapted these patterns for their own liturgical life. We know that Jesus' followers in Jerusalem 'continued to go day by day to the temple but broke the loaf in their own homes' (Acts 2.46). But here in the *Didache* – and we shall look at this in more detail in the next chapter – we see that these early communities already had a liturgical day and a liturgical week, and this new pattern of time was something that newcomers to the community had to learn to appreciate.

The day was marked by communal prayer – it was understood as communal even when someone prayed on her/his own – at three key moments. The week was marked by having two distinct days for that very visceral form of prayer: fasting. And because they were willing to fast on the Day of Preparation (i.e. Friday) they were already moving towards a week when 'the first day of the week' was going to be 'The First Day'.

Continuities

In any book on the earliest Christians it is incumbent on the writer to point out the differences between the situation in the past and today. But now, at this book's halfway mark, it is appropriate to note some continuities. We might find the demands of the *Didache* rather onerous and wonder if ever there was a community which took these seriously, so it is worth pointing out that many of these prescriptions became standard behaviour for Christians – and continued for centuries.

Obviously, the most striking continuity is that the Lord's Prayer is still at the heart of the prayer, communal and individual, of Christians. Almost no liturgical act takes place without it. Moreover, the recitation of the prayer three times a day has continued in the formal Liturgy of the Hours which is celebrated by some Christians in many traditions.

Fasting on Wednesdays and Fridays from meat, fish, dairy products, eggs, oil, wine and sex is still the official teaching governing Christians in the Orthodox world. And even though not many people follow this rule in everyday life, quite a lot do! It also became the standard practice for Latin Christians. We have a curious piece of evidence that confirms this from the Latin Church's most westerly region in the Middle Ages: Ireland. Most European languages (including Welsh which, like Irish, is a Celtic language) have the days of the week based on the Latin names linked to the seven planets. But the seven-day week arrived in Ireland with Christianity and three of the days are named from this practice of fasting. Wednesday is called *Céadaoin* which means 'first fast day', Friday is called *Aoine* which means 'the fast day', while Thursday is called *Déadaoine* which comes from 'between the two fasts'. We find it difficult to think of fasting as an act of prayer, and so we fuss about looking for moral justifications (e.g. fast and collect money not spent on food to help someone) or rationalizations (e.g. doing something 'positive' rather than 'giving something up') – forgetting that these are not either/or choices. But fasting continues to intrigue us, and has been part of many religions because it takes prayer beyond the realm of words.

Last, the notion of time as the scene in which we seek to celebrate God's presence in a distinctly Christian way, which we glimpse in the *Didache*'s instructions for the day and week, was to develop in the whole sequence of feasts and fasts that make the Christian year. Likewise, the notion of the followers of Jesus as a priestly people interceding before the Father continued in the practice of formal intercessory prayers. In many traditions this evolved to become a distinct part of the liturgy, sometimes called the 'Prayer of the Faithful', when the community calls on the Father to hear their prayer made in union with Christ.

5

Meeting and eating

The longest section of the *Didache*, apart from the Two Ways, deals with what happens when the followers of Jesus gather together and eat. This is the meal which in the second century would get the name 'the Eucharist' but which in the *Didache* is still referred to more generically with the phrase: 'now with regard to the Eucharist you should eucharistize in this way' (*Did.* 9.1). The awkwardness of the phrase shows that they did not yet think of 'the Eucharist' as the title of a distinct event, but as an action of the community; and so we should translate it as 'now this is how you should engage in giving thanks, bless God in this way . . .'. There is a difficulty in translating the related verbs '*eucharisteō*' and *eulogeō* in the first century because to 'bless God' and 'to thank God' are in effect a single reality: to say in prayer 'blessed are you for your goodness towards us' is to say 'thank you for your goodness to us' (> Audet, 1959). We need to keep this combination of meanings in mind whenever we look at first-century texts relating to the Christian meal. For example, in reading the account of the Last Supper in Luke (24.30): 'When he was at table with them, he took the loaf and blessed, and broke it, and gave it to them' – for Luke, when Jesus blessed God he was offering thanks to God. In the *Didache* we have the word *eucharisteō* pointing to both thanking and blessing (though we usually translate it as 'thanking') while in Luke's Gospel we have *eulogeō* pointing to both thanking and blessing (though we usually translate it as 'blessing').

Problems of perceptions

Reading about the eucharistic meal in the *Didache* is, for many, a most troubling experience. For some Christians today the notion that there was a formal regular meeting involving bread and wine is enough to make the whole text suspect: this is a ritual-using community that is far too 'Catholic' in its approach! For others, and these are very often Catholics, the informality of the event – clearly involving a party, with no clear directions on who presided, and, most worryingly, the absence of 'the formulae of consecration' (i.e. the phrases 'this is my body' and 'this is my blood'), have led them to assert that these chapters do not even refer to the Eucharist but to a parallel event called a 'love feast', borrowing a phrase (*agapē*) from Jude 12 where a community is chastised for 'blemishes' at its *agapē* meetings because some men are looking after themselves and not caring for others.

It is best to face these difficulties head on. First, the notion that the early communities were a 'ritual free zone' when it came to prayer ignores what we see in Judaism in the time of Jesus. Meals were times of prayer (> Finkelstein, 1929) and regular special meals, not just the Passover, were a key part of the religious tradition. No community formed from within Judaism would abandon that legacy of offering thanks to God, especially when Jesus had come proclaiming the goodness of the Father and offering thanks to the Father. Second, the notion that the Eucharist burst onto the scene at the Last Supper with a formal priesthood, specific words and a fixed theology does not allow for the fact that all religious structures change over time, evolving with some aspects becoming clearer and others more obscure. For instance, it was several centuries before the words of Jesus at the Last Supper became a standard element in a Eucharistic Prayer (> Ligier, 1973). Indeed, it would be an indication of the late date of the *Didache* if we found them there! Third, we need to recognize synonyms: the words 'agape' and 'eucharist' and 'the breaking of the loaf' (an event referred to twice in Luke's Gospel and four times in the Acts of the Apostles) all refer to the same event in the early churches. We cannot have the 'bits we like' called 'the Eucharist', while the 'bits we do not like' are all lumped together as referring to some other kind of meeting or meal (> McGowan, 1999, p. 22). We need to be open to be surprised about what all these references to the event of the Eucharist can tell us about its original significance (> Daly-Denton, 2008).

It is also worth bearing in mind two 'default settings' of human beings when it comes to religious actions. The first is this: imagining that what we saw as a child is identical with what is traditional. We have often a great fondness or a great loathing for our earliest experience of anything, and subsequently remember that as the norm from time immemorial. So if you went to church as a child and hated the ritual as long and boring, then any reference to the Eucharist in the early Church can easily provoke an allergic reaction. Likewise, if you see your first experience as basic to your faith, then you can easily imagine that that experience, with all its memories and explanations, is a norm of excellence against which every other experience is evaluated. We need to remind ourselves that religious expression is always changing even within the most rigid of traditions: new generations bring new experiences, new values and new explanations.

The second default setting is that we tend to project our concerns and debates about religious practices back to the time of the documents we use in arguments today. Thus we imagine that what worries us is what worried people 2,000 years ago. For example, for five centuries there has been a dispute among Christians over the meaning of the notion of 'grace' in St Paul. So we often read the whole of Paul as if it revolves around this sixteenth-century problem: but that is our problem, not his. It is worth remembering that people have read, and can read, Paul without even seeing this as a problem! Likewise, for 500 years there have been major divisions among Western Christians about what is the bread and wine eaten and drunk at the Eucharist and who can preside at it: but these are problems that arose from specific ways of looking at the Eucharist at specific times. They are not issues that have always been important – though those who worry about these issues find that hard to imagine – and, therefore, we should not try to answer our questions with what was said about the Eucharist by people who never thought about the Eucharist as we do. Projecting our concerns into the past as if they are absolutely essential not only twists what the past can tell us but also can blind us to how it can offer us solutions by setting our problems in perspective.

Imagining the scene

A great deal of research has taken place in recent years about the importance of meals for the early community (> Smith, 2003; or Taussig, 2009) and how those meals gave them their sense of unity with one another and with the Christ. In the meal they celebrated who they were, rejoiced in the fact that the Father loved them, and by having a meal as their basic form of gathering stressed Jesus' view of God as the loving Father who was beckoning them to the heavenly banquet. Now if we want to see how they imagined these meals together we need to look at how they remembered Jesus as the one who called people to his table and joined the tables of others, and there celebrated the Father's love. Christians have had a practice of only thinking about the Last Supper in the Synoptics (Mark 14.17–25; Matt. 26.20–29; Luke 22.14–38) as having relevance to the Eucharist, but if we want to understand the significance of the meal of the Christians (rather than one interpretation of it that later became dominant), then we need to recall just how often we see Jesus involved in dining with his disciples.

Let us look at the sequence of meals in just one Gospel: that of Luke (> Smith, 1987). Jesus dined with his disciples at Simon's house in Capernaum; his presence brought healing to Simon's mother-in-law (Luke 4.38–39). Clearly, the group around Jesus took sharing meals with him for granted: the table seems to have been his classroom in discipleship. However, dining with the tax-collector Levi when he called him to be a follower was an expression that the new kingdom would break the boundaries of existing societies (Luke 5.27–32). Part of the memory was that Jesus was prepared to keep dangerous company, and make a place for that person at his table. Jesus remained seated at table with Levi despite murmurs that he ate and drank with tax-collectors and sinners. Staying there at table is a crucial insight into the identity of Jesus.

That the kingdom of Jesus was the arrival of the great feast – the beginning of the never-ending banquet of the all-generous Father – rather than the arrival of divine punishment for sinners can also be seen in a meal (Luke 5.33–39). Jesus ate and drank with his disciples even when it scandalized the Pharisees and the disciples of John the Baptist who fasted often and offered frequent prayers. The coming of the Son of Man is not the horror of divine retribution, but begins with him eating and drinking, and inviting everyone, even the sinners, to the table (Luke 7.24–35). The theme of Jesus' shocking welcome continued when he accepted a Pharisee's hospitality and ate at his table. Then a woman from the city, a sinner, anointed his feet and wept – breaking even more boundaries – while Jesus, sitting there amid his followers, forgave her sins (Luke 7.36–50). The meal of memories was not only a place of open welcome; it was to be a place of forgiveness and reconciliation. Not only did Jesus eat at table in houses, he ate with the multitude in the wilderness. This eating showed his followers his miraculous abundance: he satisfied all with five loaves and two fish (Luke 9.10–17). Remembering the meals of the Christ meant there had to be care for all the hungry and the poor – a concern of Paul in 1 Corinthians and of the letter of Jude.

We next find Jesus sitting at table in Martha's house while her sister Mary listened to his words: once again, the teacher doing his teaching to those who sit with him – and the very act of sitting together shows the kernel of his news about a loving, welcoming Father (Luke 10.38–42). But all this teaching about table fellowship is dangerous: he dined with another Pharisee who was shocked that he did not first wash: the meal and not the law was the important thing. In the kefuffle Jesus taught them that what disqualified someone from the table of the Lord was the neglect of justice and the love of God (Luke 11.37—12.1). And he seems to have gone out of his way to share his table with those who might disapprove of him: he dined one sabbath with a ruler who was a Pharisee; then healed a man with dropsy at that meal and said, 'Blessed is the one who shall eat bread in the Kingdom of God' (Luke 14.1–24). When the good news came to Zacchaeus it came in the form of Jesus inviting himself to dinner at the man's house: it was remembered in Luke's preaching as a dinner that changed Zacchaeus' life, and brought salvation to his whole household (Luke 19.1–10).

Only when we know the story of all this eating and drinking, showing disciples, friends and even enemies the new banquet paradigm of God's love, can we start remembering when Jesus sat at table for the Passover meal, and his command to those at table to gather at a meal of a loaf and a cup in his memory (Luke 22.15–20). From the perspective of all these meals we can understand why Luke expects his hearers to understand that the disciples recognized Jesus in the breaking of the loaf at the table in Emmaus (24.13–35); and to understand that people could come from North, South, East and West to sit at table in the kingdom of God (13.29).

We have to imagine that meal in the *Didache* against the sort of background we have sketched out from just one Gospel. They gathered and shared food and taking a cup of wine – though water was used sometimes – they offered a prayer of thanks to the Father, and then taking a loaf of bread they did likewise. What set this community apart was that this sharing of food cut right across the social stratifications of the ancient world and indeed its dining practice. The poor and the rich ate together, the slaves shared a table with their masters, women ate with men, the outcasts with the religiously pure, the gentile sat next to the Jew, and all prayed to the Father and thanked him for sending his Son. Eventually this social mixing was too much for many people to take – we see the difficulties already in Corinth in the late forties (> Murphy-O'Connor, 1976 and 1977) where the rich did not want to have to share with the poor (> Theissen, 1982) – and eventually the meal would become a token affair that was wholly ritualized. Then real eating together disappeared, although the memory of that new community of love that Jesus proclaimed would always be held, at least in the imagination, by subsequent generations.

What the *Didache* says

Having dealt with fasting and prayer, the *Didache* announces its next topic:

> Now this is how you should engage in giving thanks, bless God in this way.
> First, at the cup, say:
>> We give thanks to you, our Father,
>> for the holy vine of David, your servant, which you have made known to us.
>> Through Jesus, your servant, to you be glory for ever.
>
> (*Did.* 9.1–2)

It is worth noting that Jesus is referred to as *pais* which means both 'servant' and 'son' – and we need to keep the full range of the word in mind when reading the prayer. It is rendered here as 'servant' because there is an obvious parallel being drawn between David as God's servant and Jesus as the Father's servant; and we see this also in Matthew 12.18. The *Didache* continues:

91

Then when it comes to the broken [loaf] say:
> We give thanks to you, our Father,
> for the life and knowledge which you have made known to
> us.
> Through Jesus, your servant, to you be glory for ever.
> For as the broken loaf was once scattered over the mountains
> and then was gathered in and became one, so may your
> church be gathered together into your kingdom from the very
> ends of the earth.
> Yours is the glory and the power through Jesus Christ for ever.

Only let those who have been baptized in the name of the
Lord eat and drink at your eucharists. And remember what
the Lord has said about this: do not give to dogs what is
holy.

After you all have had enough to eat, give thanks in this way:
> We give you thanks, holy Father, for your holy name which you
> have made to dwell in our hearts, and for the knowledge and
> faith and immortality which you have made known to us.
> Through Jesus, your servant, to you be glory for ever.
> You are the mighty ruler of all who has created all for your
> name's sake, and you have given food and drink to human
> beings for their enjoyment so that they might give thanks to
> you. But to us, from your generosity, you have given spirit-
> ual food and drink, and life eternal, through your servant.
> Above all things we give thanks to you because you are mighty:
> to you be glory for ever.
> Remember, Lord, your church, deliver her from evil, make
> her complete in your love, and gather her from the four winds
> into your kingdom you have prepared for her, for yours is
> the power and the glory for ever.
> May grace come and may this world pass away.
> Hosanna to the God of David.
> If anyone is holy, let him advance; if anyone is not, let him
> be converted.
> Maranatha. Amen.

However, permit the prophets to give thanks in whatever
manner they wish. (*Did.* 9.3—10.7)

Then, slightly later, we are told a few other details about the Eucharist:

> On the day which is the Day of the Lord gather together for the breaking of the loaf and giving thanks. However, you should first confess your sins so that your sacrifice may be a pure one; and do not let anyone who is having a dispute with a neighbour join until they are reconciled so that your sacrifice may not be impure.
>
> For this is the sacrifice about which the Lord has said [Mal. 1.11 and 14]: 'In every place and time let a pure sacrifice be offered to me, for I am the great king, says the Lord, and my name is feared among the nations.' (*Did.* 14)

Christians who today read these prayers, whatever tradition they come from, can find points of recognition but also items that surprise, some because of their inclusion and some because they are not included. When we look at it as a single piece of teaching rather than as bits, however, it has the ability to generate some fundamental questions for every Christian assembly today.

What the *Didache* tells us

The *Didache* gave the person who committed it to memory the basic forms for prayers needed for the Christian meal. It does not give a narrator's description such as we might get if there had been someone at such a meal acting as a reporter. Nor does it give a normative format for the meal as if this was the one-and-only way to have such a meal. If there is a prophet present (important people in the world of the early Christians) then he was to say whatever prayers he thought best (*Did.* 10.7). This means that trying to fit the pattern of what we find in the *Didache* into patterns relating to later practice is always difficult: they did not write for us but for themselves and they assumed familiarity with the actual practice. So, on many topics that interest us, they simply took practice for granted. Therefore, rather than trying to link what we think was the actual practice with what developed later in details (> Stewart-Sykes, 2004, for example), let us note some of the most prominent assumptions and understandings.

The most striking feature is that the Eucharist is part of a real meal. This was a continuation of the meal practice of Jesus: the disciples become the assembly around the table and there bless the Father in the way that they believed Jesus did. We are given no details about who brought the food, where the meal took place, whether it was an evening meal or at some other time. We are given simply a set of sample prayers for blessing the Father, that offer thanks in the midst of celebrating his goodness, and we can assume, thereby, the fact that the new community gathered for this meal. This gathering cannot have been easy for them. While banquets were part of ancient culture, these were very stratified affairs where social relationships were clearly maintained and, indeed, reaffirmed. Here we have just the instruction that the meal is confined to those who have entered the community of Jesus through baptism. All that we saw the *Didache* saying of baptism now becomes practice. Baptism marked the boundary of the community. The Eucharist shows the community assembled and becomes the practice that maintains the community. In short, if you are a follower of Jesus on the Way, then you have a place at this table. At this table, the good things of earth are shared by all, and the Father is thanked for his heavenly goodness, his supreme gift, the Christ.

The name Christians give to their celebration is 'eucharist' – thanksgiving – and this was equivalent to 'blessing God' – which we see Jesus doing – which is declaring how great and good God is for all his wonderful gifts to us. This aspect of praising God for his goodness is often just one theme among many in later practice, but here it is clearly to the fore. God, now understood as the Father who has sent his servant/child among us, is thanked for all the goodness of the creation, and then thanked for the gift beyond all that is in the creation. Thankful for the food and drink that give human joy, Christians are distinctly grateful for the food and drink of eternal life (*Did.* 10.3). This is the food and drink that is given through Jesus. This notion that Jesus gives eternal life through a gift we eat and drink finds echoes in John's preaching: to the woman of Samaria Jesus offers the water of eternal life (John 4.14) and his Father gives the true manna that gives immortality (John 6.31–33). To share in the meal was to receive the greatest gift of the Father – to have a share in eternal life, through Jesus. So, at this meal there was food for the body and earthly enjoyment and there was food for eternal life and the enjoyment of the life of heaven – and all because of the life and knowledge that came through Jesus. No fewer than four times (*Did.* 9.2, 3, 4, 10.2) do we find this refrain: what we do in thanking, that we are able to thank the Father and that we are able to rejoice in the Father's goodness, is because we are praying 'through Jesus, your servant/child'.

One of the distinguishing features of the meals of Jesus was that he took a cup and, having blessed the Father, shared it with his disciples. This is a ritual without parallel in the ancient world: it is one thing to offer a thanksgiving over a cup – and by extension over all the cups of the participants of the meal – but quite another to pass a single cup from one to another. Yet here we find this practice: to share a cup is to assert an intimate unity and a common purpose. The disciples have to be prepared to drink from the cup of Jesus (> Mark 10.38–39) and thereby they share in his destiny. At the meal in the *Didache* one of the rituals is that the single cup of the Lord is shared by all those at the meal. One cup is unity, and it cuts across every human boundary and division – it is not accidental that Christians have always tried to find ways around sharing the cup in their celebrations! Likewise, they offered thanks over a broken loaf. The loaf that is shared is a basic symbol of togetherness around a table. We still eat shares of a birthday cake – and so celebrate with the person whose birthday is being celebrated. We share a wedding cake to celebrate with the couple – even sending little portions to those who cannot get to the wedding so that they can be linked with the party. And Jesus is remembered as having broken and shared a loaf with his disciples. The loaf broken into pieces allows each to have a piece, and eating shares of the single loaf makes each person at table a part of that one loaf. This sharing of a cup and a loaf is the basic ritual that underlies all the ways that early Christians sought to explain what the meal meant for them (> Nodet and Taylor, 1998, pp. 88–126).

This aspect of the Eucharist, that it involved sharing a single cup and breaking a loaf so that each has a share, has been obscured for us by our fascination with what it is we receive in 'holy communion': and so endless debates over bread and wine and whether they are or become the body and blood of Christ. But this later debate focuses on a type of food, bread, whereas the early concern was with the actual object one takes in one's hands: a loaf of bread. Likewise, there was so little concern with 'what one drinks' that many early communities used water (> McGowan, 1999): the key concern was with how one drinks from a single cup passed from one to another. However, we can see the power of later ideas in the fact that most translators of the *Didache*, as indeed of the New Testament books, still translate what Jesus took in his hands as 'bread' (i.e. thinking in the medieval categories of what it *is*) rather than as 'loaf' (i.e. thinking in terms of what the action of sharing it among those at the table means). The *Didache* forcefully reminds us that when we read any early account of the Christian meal, the focus is on many sharing a single cup and eating shares of a single loaf (> O'Loughlin 2003b, and 2004).

So how did they draw out further meanings from this practice? Let us begin with how Paul interpreted sharing a loaf and cup in 1 Corinthians before looking at the different take we find in the *Didache*'s prayers.

Paul writes:

> The cup of blessing that we bless, is it not a sharing in the blood
> of Christ? The loaf that we break, is it not a sharing in the body
> of Christ? Because there is one loaf, we who are many are one
> body, for we all partake of the one bread . . . You cannot drink
> the cup of the Lord and the cup of demons. You cannot partake
> of the table of the Lord and the table of demons.
>
> (1 Cor. 10.16–17 and 21 [NRSV, adapted])

Here, the fact of one cup and one loaf is above all pointing
to unity and union. To share the cup and loaf means that
the community are one body; they are united by this eating
and drinking. Moreover, to share this cup and loaf brings
about union with the Lord, in just the same way that sharing
in food offered to the demons would link the participants
with them. Those who gather for the Christian meal are made
into one body and that is the body of Christ. In the *Didache*
we see a different take on the ritual. Israel saw itself as having
been scattered and one of the actions of the Anointed One
would be to gather all these scattered individuals and reunite
them as one people. We see it in texts like these from the
prophets:

> Hear the word of the LORD, O nations, and declare it in the
> coastlands far away; say, 'He who scattered Israel will gather
> him, and will keep him as a shepherd a flock'.
>
> (Jer. 31.10 [NRSV]);

or:

> Thus says the Lord GOD: When I gather the house of Israel from
> the peoples among whom they are scattered, and manifest my
> holiness in them in the sight of the nations, then they shall
> settle on their own soil that I gave to my servant Jacob.
>
> (Ezek. 28.25 [NRSV])

Now the community believed that this process of gathering
was taking place through Jesus the good shepherd – and it was

taking place in their meal. The loaf was itself a symbol of gathering: it started off as seeds that were scattered, then they were gathered and transformed into the unity that is the loaf – and now each is sharing in that unity at the meal that anticipates the heavenly banquet. For Paul the meal's ritual shows that we are one, new people; for the *Didache* it shows that we have been gathered up by the Messiah to become the new people. Scattered to the four winds, they are now gathered, transformed into a holy people, and made part of the kingdom (*Did.* 10.5).

And when the gathered people bless the Father and offer thanks 'through Jesus' they are offering the sacrifice that is pure and holy: the praise and thanksgiving of the Messiah's people. So sharing in the meal requires that they acknowledge their sins and in that act of acknowledging their sinfulness is the acceptance of the Father's forgiveness; and so there must be a concurrent acknowledgement of quarrels and a seeking of reconciliation. Just as a difficulty with God makes sharing the meal inappropriate so does a difficulty with a neighbour. So both vertical and horizontal relationships need to be repaired and then the sacrifice is worthy. There is a linking of the need to be reconciled with God (*Did.* 14.1) and to be reconciled with neighbour (*Did.* 14.2) that is exactly parallel to the prayer for forgiveness in the Lord's Prayer where we ask to be forgiven by God for our trespasses against him *just as* we forgive the neighbours who trespass against us. The meal in its totality is, therefore, a sacrifice of praise to the Father. Moreover, as the perfect sacrifice, made in union with Jesus, it fulfils the prophecy of perfect sacrifice, that one, perfect sacrifice that would be offered from the rising of the sun to its setting (Mal. 1.11–14/*Did.* 14.3).

Therefore, we can say that the Christian meal:

- forms a communion of all who share it and they become the one, reunited people;

- makes a communion of them with Jesus whose meal it is and in whose life they share;
- joins them as one in the perfect sacrifice;
- and so joins them with all the other groups of Christians from east to west who are gathering for this meal;
- and joins them, through Christ, with the Father sharing in his gifts of life and immortality.

We often use the phrase 'holy communion' for the Eucharist. In the *Didache* we see the full range of meanings that should come to mind: the meal celebrates the communion of the gathering with one another, communion with all Christians, communion with Christ and communion with the Father.

How often did they meet?

We have seen that the *Didache* took over the liturgical week from Judaism and transformed it (> ch. 4); we see here that the sabbath's eve was replaced by a gathering on 'the Day of the Lord' (Sunday). So the meal took place at least weekly, but it may have been more frequent in that there is no hint in the *Didache* that every meal of Christians could not have been considered eucharistic. If all knew the prayers of thanks (think of the parallel with 'grace' before and after meals) then at each meal a cup could have been blessed and a loaf broken. Certainly, we should not just think of elaborate banquets: many poor communities would have had difficulties having even a weekly festive meal, and wine was not ubiquitous but a drink that required some wealth. We can imagine communities where the majority were slaves or poor people and the cup and loaf of the Eucharist were combined with a very ordinary meal indeed. It is in this context that we have to recall that while we think of the cup as filled with wine, with all its rich symbolism, this only became a standard element when the Eucharist had become a ritual distinct from the common meal of the new people. Jesus had welcomed all to his table, so every table of Christians could have held the promise of the kingdom (> Jewett, 1994).

Who led the meal?

One of the most troubling questions for many modern Christians concerns who can lead the Eucharist; and then this becomes questions about who has the 'power to consecrate' and whether or not there is a Eucharist if there is no one who is ordained. All such questions assume that the Eucharist is an event one attends rather than an activity engaged in by Christians when they gather. Alas for those looking for neat confirmations of their doctrinal positions from history, the *Didache* does not oblige and it provides no clear answers to the burning questions of later times. The *Didache*, as we shall see in the next chapter, does show us that the communities that used it had leaders, but the only comment about who offers the blessing at the meal is that a 'prophet' can use whatever formula he wishes. There is simply no indication that the one who said the prayers was a presbyter – the word that gives us the word 'priest' – or a bishop. Now, immediately some either jump to the conclusion that it must have been only priests – because in later times a priest was a 'must' for a Eucharist – or jump even further beyond the evidence and suggest that if there was no mention of a priest then this is not a description of a 'real' Eucharist! These sorts of argument all share a common element: they assume that what is declared to be doctrinally necessary at a later date must also be in historical continuity with the earliest practice. However, it is actually a rare event when doctrinal 'musts' match historical 'facts' exactly (> Frend, 2003) – this is a mismatch that Christians today taking 'all-or-nothing' positions on many aspects of Church practice might keep in mind.

We can imagine a situation like this in those early decades. At the Sunday gathering whoever was considered one of the leaders of the community – and remember this took place in a house so it would not have been a large gathering – took the lead in making the thanksgiving at the meal. But at other times, whoever was the head of the table – the householder – took the lead. So when one Christian hosted a meal for other Christians, that person took the lead. The assumption of the *Didache* is that every Christian should know these prayers for celebrating a eucharistic meal – perhaps the ideal it aspired to was that no meal would be shared without the Father being thanked for his gifts and his gift of Jesus – and so we can assume that every Christian was expected to have use of this skill from time to time. Indeed, if the 'prophets' – who seem to have been the experts in the Way (> ch. 6) – are allowed to use whatever form of prayer they wish, then the fact that these prayers are laid out in full presumes that everyone else needed a learned formula; this in turn presumes that every Christian may have use for such a formula.

The Last Supper

One other issue needs to be raised: when most Christians think of the origins of the Eucharist they think of the scene of the final dinner in three of the Gospels (Mark, Matthew and Luke) and this often prompts the question as to why there is no mention of the Last Supper in the *Didache*. While we should note that this is an anachronistic question – it was several centuries before a reference to the Last Supper became a standard part of eucharistic prayers – it is still worth noting the question as it can throw additional light on the practices of the earliest churches. In Mark's Gospel, the Eucharist is presented as being given to the disciples at a Passover meal (Mark 14.12) – and such a meal was an annual event. However, the general Christian practice has been to celebrate the eucharistic meal at least weekly – and the *Didache* is our earliest witness to this practice. Indeed, those churches today that hold the Eucharist less frequently than once a week are inheriting a sixteenth-century practice which argued that if the Eucharist began at the Passover then it should be an annual event or, at least, an infrequent event.

So we have a strange situation: the communities to which Mark, Matthew and Luke were preaching were gathering weekly (and it was probably at these weekly gatherings that these men were preaching their Gospels), yet when it came to the part of the *kerugma* that dealt with the meal for which they were gathered they heard about it in terms of an annual celebration. How can this situation be accounted for?

We have seen that the meal practice of the churches is not some formal obedience to a command, 'do this', but emerged out of continuity with the meal practice of Jesus. It is this continuity of practice that is at the core of the Eucharist: they thanked the Father, they shared a cup, they shared a loaf, they rejoiced at who they had been called to become. It is within this continuity of practice that all the explanations of the Eucharist emerged. We have seen how one such explanation can be found in Paul, another in the *Didache*, and yet another can be found in Mark when he places the Eucharist within the context of the climax of his Gospel. For Mark the meal reminds us that Jesus is our passover lamb, and the meal is a sharing in his life, death and resurrection.

The meal with its blessing and special forms of sharing is the continuity: the explanations – whether in Paul, the *Didache* or the Gospel – are all building up and drawing out the implications of that meal. We can see these various explanations as 'theologies': expressions of what it means to share this meal. Each draws out from experience a different aspect, and the well of such explanations seems to be inexhaustible!. So we should look on Mark's story of the Last Supper as a way of linking a basic fact of his audience's experience into the Gospel's story. It is repeated, but with different emphases, in the Gospel of Matthew and in the Gospel of Luke. While John in his Gospel has a Last Supper, he has no mention of the Eucharist on that evening: but rather locates the Eucharist experience of his audience in a series of signs and stories in Galilee (John 6—7) and after the resurrection (John 20—21) – this is something we also find in Luke (Luke 24.28–35) and in a few other stories that have survived from early Church circles (> O'Loughlin, 2009). As we saw in Chapter 3 when looking at baptism, it is the event – the actual baptism, the actual eating of the meal at table – that formed the basis of Christian practice. Explanations came afterwards and can be seen as providing a range of answers to the question: why do we do this?

Around a table

Nothing bonds us as human beings like sharing a meal: we are the only animals who cook our food – and this indicates that eating is always something more significant to us than just inputting nourishment. Around the table we become families, friends and communities. Meals mark what is significant in life: a life without festive meals marking the events of our lives would point to a very dull life indeed. Meals make us human.

Meals also are at the heart of many religions: the harvest is celebrated because working together we have ensured the continuity of life and that famine will not overtake us. Eating together we recall all that is most important to us and celebrate it: the banquet is a basic form of ritual when we affirm who we are, recall our stories and set out our hopes and desires. The People of Israel had a rich inheritance of such special meals: celebrating the various moments of the harvest and linking to them the mighty works of God that made them his people. Whether it was the great annual meal of the Passover or the meal on the eve of the sabbath, on each occasion God was blessed: praised and thanked for his goodness using a pattern of prayers. Jesus took over these practices, while also transforming them. The table would be inclusive – the welcome he extended would be as open as that extended by the Father to humanity – and would be a place to discover the goodness and generosity of the Father. There he would show his followers a new way of blessing the Father and of demonstrating their communion. This meal practice was continued by the disciples, and around the table they discovered that in this meal they were united with one another and with Jesus, the servant of the Father, and through him they were offering in their meal the perfect sacrifice. This meal not only echoes with the new vision of God and his relationship to his people that Jesus preached, but it demonstrated in the intimacy of sharing a cup and loaf the new structures of humanity: poor eating with rich, slaves with slave owners, men with women, gentiles with Jews. The breaching of the boundaries of Graeco-Roman society at this Christian meal is one of the miracles of the early Church. Later, it would all seem too much and the meal would be replaced with a token eating and drinking, it would become obscured under competing explanations – and eventually we would end up with the irony that the meal that is intended to unite Christians has become one of their main points of argument and division. But dating from before all those later changes we have the *Didache*, offering us a precious insight into the meal in the earliest communities and reminding us how it was a central event in shaping disciples.

6

A network of service

The Christian churches are among the oldest organizations in the world. Over centuries they have developed systems of enormous diversity and complexity with bureaucracies, legal systems and communications networks that reach all over the globe. For some people all these hierarchies – note the word began within a church setting – and structures are a source of amazement: they live their lives within them, are formed by them, and are even sometimes more attentive to these systems than they are to the gospel these structures exist to serve. For others, these same structures are like millstones around the necks of Christians and are the antithesis of the gospel. Structures, they feel, are not only distractions but often replace the message of Jesus with a life-diminishing system of regulations that are more concerned with preserving power than reflecting the life-giving Spirit. But between those who embrace religious structures and those who detest them stands a simple fact: all human communities need structures. Structures are necessary both to enable a community to live in harmony and to ensure that it is not broken up by disputes. We see both of these concerns in the *Didache*. The community wants to make sure that it is not led astray by false teachers, yet also that it treats teachers properly, and that it asks the right questions about those whom it calls to specific tasks within the community.

Since long before the *Didache* was discovered in 1873, one of the questions about the earliest Christians that has exercised scholars has been the 'church order' question. By this they meant the question of the origins of what most churches today still see as the essential core of their leadership structures, the 'three-fold ministry' of bishops, presbyters and deacons. The churches who use these structures claim that it goes back to the time of the apostles, indeed to Jesus himself, yet the earliest references to such ministers do not follow the later pattern or else are in problematic documents (e.g. 1 Tim., 2 Tim. and Titus) in that they date from long after the time of Paul. The pattern only becomes clear with the writings of Ignatius of Antioch (early second century; > Foster, 2006) and even then we do not know how universal was Ignatius's ideal pattern. But even if clarity came in the early second century that still left a gap of many decades that some people were anxious to bridge so that there would be a clear line of 'apostolic succession' from the Twelve to those second-century bishops. In this quest the focus of any examination was not to look at any particular text and see what it tells us about the community's structures but to examine each as an 'anticipation' for what later became both normal and normative. Hence many studies of the *Didache* see it as but a moment in a process to where things ultimately led. This is fine if one's question is focused on the origins of later structures (> Sullivan, 2001, pp. 81–102), or if one is trying to justify a particular pattern as 'the only valid system'; but here I shall adopt another approach. Here the focus is upon the communities that used the *Didache*: their problems and their concerns, and what these can tell us about the life of the early Christian movement in the first century.

The *Didache* supposed a closely knit community where everyone would have known the other people in the community and where all could have assembled for the eucharistic meal. Hence we are thinking of a community of no more than a hundred people, and probably less. It is important to keep this question of size in the forefront of our minds as we read the *Didache*, as it is one thing to think of a single bishop (another second-century development) or a group of bishops (our earliest references to bishops is as a group with the compound title 'bishops and deacons', as we shall see further on) in a community of a hundred people, and quite another to think of a bishop who is at the head of a modern diocese with thousands of people and umpteen professional ministers. The situation in the *Didache* is vastly different. In a human-sized community – something that is always around 150 people maximum – there were several men known as 'bishops and deacons'. This brings to mind the image of servants of the community; it was a situation that could not be scaled-up without the inevitable transformation of those servants into managers of plant, personnel and policy.

Another issue to keep in mind when reading the *Didache* is one's image of 'the church'. For some Christians this is primarily an international organization and they either do not use the term for an actual community or else use some term like 'the local church' which is then thought of as the equivalent to the local branch of other global organizations. For other Christians 'the church' is the actual community to which they belong, and 'the Church' above and beyond these communities is a less tangible reality and is more like a federation of local clubs. The first model, favoured by Catholics and some Anglicans, is really a product of medieval canon law: where each diocese is constituted by its relationship to a centre, while smaller units, 'parishes', are often thought of as geographical service points. The second model, favoured mainly by Protestants, is a product of the Reformation: the community is the church and wider structures are based either on political unities or on federation. Neither model is useful when we read the *Didache* for it predates the developments that produced our dominant models.

When reading the *Didache* we have to keep in mind two distinct ideas simultaneously. On the one hand, they knew that they belonged to an actual community: into such a community they were baptized; that community ate together, heard visiting prophets, alerted itself to false prophets and frauds, and it was that group that appointed for itself 'bishops and deacons' (literally: 'overseers and servants') (*Did.* 15.1); and it would appear that these were not two separate offices but that there were several men who functioned as 'bishop-deacons' to the community. On the other hand, they were part of the new people of Jesus and as such were united with every other Christian. This larger unity was not just notional but made itself felt in many ways. Churches welcomed visitors from other churches; there were itinerant prophets and teachers; apostles moved around; and evangelists went from church to church preaching 'the gospel' (the recordings on papyrus of these preachers would become our four Gospels). This network also extended to money – there was a collection organized by Paul among churches in Greece to provide support after a famine in Palestine – and to books: the texts of letters were read in churches to which they were not originally addressed and the texts of the Gospels were read in communities that may never have heard one of the Gospels from the lips of one of the evangelists. We often use the slogan 'think global, act local'. For the early churches it was more complex: they had to think and act local *while* thinking and acting global.

Networks

The first followers of Jesus lived close to the edge of the Graeco-Roman world. Stretching out to the west was the Greek-speaking world of the Mediterranean, stretching out to the east were regions that spoke Syriac, and beyond Syria lay the Persian empire and then the lands of India. South lay Arabia, and south of Alexandria lay Coptic-speaking Egypt, and beyond that lay Ethiopia. To the northwest, beyond the Greek-speaking areas (which could be found as far west as the Rhône valley in modern France) lay the Latin-speaking world. From scattered references it would appear that Christians spread in all these directions, but it is only from the Hellenistic world, the Greek-speaking areas around the Mediterranean, that we have early documents.

Indeed, all the early documents we have originated in that world, and then were translated from Greek into the various languages of the east, or Africa, or elsewhere. Therefore, it is from the networks of that Mediterranean world that we have to build up our picture of early churches (see Figure 6.1 overleaf).

By the time of Jesus there was already a scattering of Jews across that world. Alexandria was a great centre of Jewish learning and it was probably there that the Scriptures were translated into Greek – and this collection (rather than the shorter list of books that became normative in Judaism after the destruction of the Temple in AD 70) would become the Old Testament of the Christians. There were synagogues across the region we now call Turkey in Asia, and around the Aegean. There were synagogues in Italy (> Aharoni et al., 2003, p. 81) and by the early second century there were synagogues as far west as present-day Marseille and Toledo (> Aharoni et al., 2003, p. 104). This was 'the *diaspora*' (the dispersion; > John 7.35) and these Jews maintained links with the Temple in Jerusalem. It was this network of synagogues that Paul used when he was on his journeys announcing Jesus (> Acts 13.5, for example).

The new communities soon added networks of their own. Jesus gathered around him as his core group 'the Twelve'. But already by the time Mark was preaching his Gospel (the 60s of the first century) these were being identified as 'the apostles' (> Mark 3.14), as it was taken for granted in the churches that the leaders were 'those sent out' (the literal meaning of 'apostles') to go from church to church preaching. They saw their task as announcing that 'the time' when God had finally shown his hand in history had arrived (> Meier, 2001, pp. 40–197). But there were many others, not just Paul and his companions, whose existence we glimpse in passing references: moving from place to place, establishing communities, teaching those groups, providing links between them, and giving them the sense that they formed this new community that broke existing boundaries of race and class.

Figure 6.1 The eastern Mediterranean in the first century AD
This shows the Graeco-Roman cities with Christian communities in the first century: these churches formed a network with evangelists, apostles, prophets and other Christians moving between them. The *Didache* was not only diffused via this network but also provided guidance about the people moving within it.

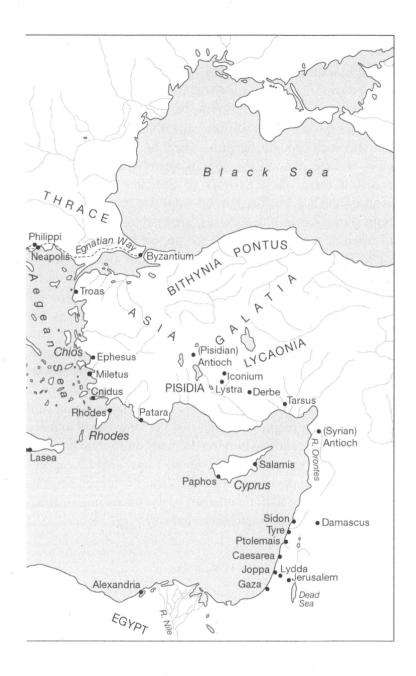

But how difficult would all this travelling have been? The sea was the great highway of the Greek world: that is why its culture had spread far and wide; it was the basis of the Athenian empire centuries earlier; and it was the basis of long-range trade such as that which brought Egyptian wheat to feed the burgeoning cities of Italy. Around the Aegean where we know from Paul and Acts there was a network of churches in the mid-first century, the sea was the normal route for most communications. From Corinth to Ephesus, for example, took from four to seven days going east (with the prevailing wind) and from six to ten days going west. From Ephesus to Troas took from two to three days going south (with the wind) and from five to seven days going north. From these coastal cities there were roads, some much older than those built by the Romans, that linked inland cities. A journey from Troas to Antioch in Syria, going via Tarsus, Paul's home city, would have taken about six weeks (the sea journey would have taken about three weeks). From Antioch to Jerusalem would have taken eighteen days by land and perhaps half that by sea – but someone going from group to group might have preferred the longer land journeys as it would have allowed him to visit many more churches along the way (> Thompson, 1998). So all these Christian groups were not only linked by shared beliefs and a common language but also had these links maintained by visitors taking advantage of the imperial communications' network.

Teachers

Conscious of all this movement between Christian communities, we can now read the instructions of the *Didache* on the matter.

> Now, whoever comes to you and teaches all these things which have just been set out here, you are to welcome him.
> However, if a teacher has himself wandered from the right path and has begun to teach a teaching that is at odds with what is set out here, you should not listen to him.

On the other hand, if his teaching promotes holiness and knowledge of the Lord, then you should welcome him as you would the Lord. (*Did.* 11.1–2)

The community sees itself as having the duty to offer welcome and hospitality (> Riddle, 1938). And it welcomes good teachers 'as if the Lord' himself had come among them. This notion of welcoming someone 'as if he were the Lord' was clearly a core value for the churches as we find the theme expressed in the Gospels and linked to Jesus himself: 'Truly, truly, I say to you, he who receives any one whom I send receives me; and he who receives me receives him who sent me' (John 13.20 [RSV]); and there are similar ideas in the other evangelists (> Mark 9.37; Matt. 10.40; Luke 9.48). We are given no clue about what these teachers did except that they were to teach the same teaching as the *Didache* – so presumably these were people with special communications skills such as the preacher's skills of persuasive speech, or they may have had that rare ability to promote holiness/righteousness (*dikaiosunē*) and knowledge of the Lord in the community. It would seem, from the fact that teachers are mentioned in the *Didache* before anyone else, that these were the most common of the travellers that were going from church to church. Paul, writing in the mid-50s to the Corinthians to point out that the Spirit gives a variety of gifts, says:

And God has appointed in the church first apostles, second prophets, third teachers, then workers of miracles, then healers, helpers, administrators, speakers in various kinds of tongues. Are all apostles? Are all prophets? Are all teachers? Do all work miracles? Do all possess gifts of healing? Do all speak with tongues? Do all interpret? (1 Cor. 12.28–30 [RSV])

It is with just the first three groups, all of which are forms of service inspired by the Spirit, that there is concern in the *Didache*.

But two other points should be noted before we read more of the *Didache*. First, we are inclined to think of the early

Church in romantic terms: then all were devoted, all were sincere, and all was well. We know from the arguments recorded in the letters of Paul, who had to upbraid the Corinthians and oppose Peter (> Gal. 2.11), and Acts, which tells the tale of Simon the magician who wanted to buy 'power' from the apostles (8.9–24), that there were problems right from the start. We see similar problems in the *Didache*. It is a concern of the *Didache* to distinguish true from false teachers: true teachers are in harmony with the *Didache*'s own teaching while listening to them promotes Christian growth. But there were also frauds: those who had gone astray from the Way, and they are to be recognized by the fact that what they say is different from the *Didache*'s teaching. We see the same concern with those who preach a different gospel to what Paul himself preached when he wrote to the Galatians (> Gal 1.7–11) around the same time as he was writing to the Corinthians. We will see other concerns about false visitors again further on in the *Didache*.

Second, we live in a literate culture: we all read books, papers and information on the internet – and absorb it for ourselves through *reading*. However, ancient culture was aural: you listened to speech, you heard speech that had been recorded in marks on papyrus and converted back in sounds by a reader. Note that teaching is not something you read, but something to which you listen (> Achtemeier, 1990). There is always a real community of a teacher speaking and a disciple or disciples listening. We see this aural culture in Paul's statement: 'So faith comes from what is heard, and what is heard comes through the word of Christ' (Rom. 10.17 [NRSV]). Moreover, it should remind us not to push our assumptions about reading, which is essentially a private activity, and books back into this period. The *Didache* was a document that was memorized and heard – and also had its sounds recorded on papyrus for safekeeping; the epistles were speeches whose sound was recorded so that it could go where their writers could not go; and the Gospels were the recordings of the evangelists which enabled them to be heard again and again after the evangelist himself had moved on.

Apostles and prophets

When we think of the term 'apostle' we tend to think of the Twelve – the disciples around Jesus, many of whose names we think we know – rather than the larger group mentioned by Paul when he wrote to the Corinthians, but unless we recall this larger group moving around the churches we cannot understand the seemingly harsh instructions of the *Didache*:

> Now, turning to apostles and prophets you must treat them according to the rule of the gospel.
> Every apostle who arrives among you is to be welcomed as if he were the Lord.
> But normally he must not stay with you for more than one day, but he may stay a second day if this is necessary. However, if he stays a third day, then he is a false prophet!
> When he leaves you, an apostle must receive nothing except enough food to sustain him until the next night's lodgings. However, if he asks for money, then he is a false prophet!
>
> (*Did.* 11.3–6)

Religion seems to attract charlatans, then as now: people who want to make a living out of the generosity of God and his people. The *Didache* takes the clearest line possible: no money and only the food needed to perform the task involved and get the apostle to the next community – anything more and they are loafers. Seen in this light we see the actual situation among the churches that may lie behind the statement put into the mouth of Jesus by Luke when 'the seventy' – who seem to be the prototypical apostles – were sent out without purse or bag and told to 'remain in the same house, eating and drinking what they provide, for the labourer deserves his wages; do not go from house to house' (Luke 10.7 [RSV]) – significantly the only 'wage' they are entitled to is their lodging, food and drink (which is exactly what the *Didache* prescribes). This issue of false apostles and those making a quick buck out of the gospel was obviously a contentious one in the early churches. Paul takes the position that an apostle is entitled to a wage – presumably board and lodging – but is so concerned that his preaching might be impugned by taking even that which was his right that he chose to support himself, and probably his wife, by carrying on his trade. He told the Thessalonians:

> For you remember our labour and toil, brethren; we worked night and day, that we might not burden any of you, while we preached to you the gospel of God.   (1 Thess. 2.9 [RSV])

He repeated it later:

> [W]e did not eat anyone's bread without paying, but with toil and labour we worked night and day, that we might not burden any of you. It was not because we have not that right, but to give you in our conduct an example to imitate.
> (1 Thess. 3.8–9 [RSV])

While to the Corinthians – to whom he wanted to prove his authority – he wrote:

> Do we not have the right to be accompanied by a wife, as the other apostles and the brothers of the Lord and Cephas? Or is it only Barnabas and I who have no right to refrain from working for a living? . . . If others share this rightful claim upon you, do not we still more?
> Nevertheless, we have not made use of this right, but we endure anything rather than put an obstacle in the way of the gospel of Christ . . . What then is my reward? Just this: that in my preaching I may make the gospel free of charge, not making full use of my right in the gospel.
> (1 Cor. 9.5–6, 12, 18 [RSV])

What exactly 'the rule of the gospel' was with regard to apostles is unclear – there is no statement mentioned in the four Gospels that could be construed as being a rule – but the most likely statement we have (remember that the 'good news' cannot simply be identified with our four Gospels) is that the rule is that apostles should be welcomed as if it were the Lord himself: 'He who receives you receives me, and he who receives me receives him who sent me' (Matt. 10.40 [RSV]). However, while the 'rule' may be uncertain, that there was a concern over the arrival of false prophets among the early churches is clearly shown in our four Gospels, when this statement is put into the mouth of Jesus by Matthew: 'Beware of false prophets, who come to you in sheep's clothing but inwardly are ravenous wolves. You will know them by their fruits. Are grapes gathered from thorns, or figs from thistles?' (Matt. 7.15–16 [RSV]).

Testing prophets

The statement that 'you will know them by their fruits' was a touchstone for the communities of the *Didache* in making sure that they did not become victims of fraud or get saddled with ministers who were out for themselves. Its instructions are clear, precise and sensible – and many distractions and much nonsense would have been kept out of Christianity over the centuries if these guidelines had been strictly applied to clergy:

> Now if any prophet speaks in the Spirit he is not to be tested: for every sin can be forgiven but this sin cannot be forgiven.
> However, not everyone who speaks in the Spirit is a prophet: only those who show that they follow the Way of the Lord. It is by the way that he lives that the true prophet can be separated from the false one.
> Now if a prophet speaking in the Spirit orders a banquet, then that man should not partake in it; if he does eat the meal, then he is a false prophet.
> And any prophet who teaches the truth, but does not live according to his teaching is to be considered a false prophet.
> . . .

> Now if anyone should say in the Spirit 'Give me money' – or
> anything like that – you should not listen to that man; however,
> if he tells you to give something to other people who are in need,
> then he is not to be condemned. (*Did.* 11.7–10, 12)

Speaking in tongues, here referred to as 'speaking in the Spirit',
was a feature of the early communities that was seen as being
open to abuse or of being an end in itself. Paul was concerned
that 'tongues' might be seen as sufficient, without love, to
exhibit life in Christ (1 Cor. 13.1) and also points out that
'tongues' is a useless gift without interpretation to build up the
Church (1 Cor. 14.5–6). This same balance is to be seen here
in the *Didache*: you must not dismiss tongues, because they are
a gift of the Spirit, but at the same time there must be no false
opposition between the teaching and tongues: anyone who
speaks in tongues must also be an adherent of the Way of Life.
Paul has almost an echo of the *Didache* when he, rather than
speaking in tongues, asks the Corinthians: 'how shall I benefit
you unless I bring you some revelation or knowledge or prophecy or teaching?' (1 Cor. 14.6 [rsv]). The test of speaking in
the Spirit is that the speaker knows and lives by the *didache*.
Moreover, it is easy to spot the conman: he orders a free meal
'in the Spirit'. The *Didache* has almost a touch of humour in
its reply: yes, let him order it, but if he is genuine, then he will
not want to eat it himself. For a prophet to benefit himself
would undermine his credibility – even if he did genuinely
speak in the Spirit, when he asked that a table be laid – and
this is probably the background to Paul's not even taking the
food to which he is entitled from the community but rather
working to pay for his own upkeep: by getting no benefit, he
was stressing that his service was genuine.

The final note is interesting in that it sets the actual walking
of the Way as a test for anyone who acts as a prophet. The
correct teaching is not enough in itself, it must be backed up
by the correct form of life. The *Didache* has a bald statement
intended as a test for the community to use to distinguish

visitors in two groups: false and genuine. The same basic teaching comes in a more nuanced form in a scene in Matthew's Gospel, where Jesus tells the crowds and the disciples that the scribes and Pharisees preach the law (and so they should be listened to) but do not practise it (and so should not be imitated). In his community all were to be brothers, and he would be the only teacher (23.1–8). Just as the *Didache* is concerned with charlatans living off the communities, Matthew seems concerned about those who are seeking positions of power and respect within those communities.

In Mark's Gospel we hear a very strange utterance from Jesus that has baffled interpreters down the centuries: 'Truly, I say to you, all sins will be forgiven the sons of men, and whatever blasphemies they utter; but whoever blasphemes against the Holy Spirit never has forgiveness, but is guilty of an eternal sin' (3.28–29 [RSV]) – and Matthew follows Mark but with a slightly different emphasis (Matt. 12.31). Here we see the same teaching in the *Didache*: all sins can be forgiven except that of casting doubt on the fact of a prophet speaking in the Spirit. In the Gospels the blasphemy consists in denying that the Spirit is working in the Christ, here that the Spirit is working in the prophets. The *Didache*'s sense of the seriousness of this sin is inexplicable: it neither helps us understand the Gospels nor do the Gospels help us to understand the *Didache*. It is a reminder that there are many instances where we do not really know what was happening in the world of the early churches: often we can make sound conjectures, and sometimes, as here, we have simply to note our ignorance. Some people find admitting such ignorance difficult and scramble for an explanation to cover 'the gap'; such attempts not only pretend to understanding we do not have but also have the effect of bringing what we do know into disrepute.

The issue of 'the unforgivable sin' is not the only topic where the *Didache*'s concern about the behaviour of prophets is obscure. Here is an instruction which has not only baffled modern scholars but was already beyond the understanding of those who translated the *Didache* into Ethiopian and Georgian – and who were much closer to the world in which it was written (> Niederwimmer, 1998, pp. 180–2):

> Any prophet, who has been proven to be a true prophet, who acts out in his life the earthly mystery of the church (provided that he does not teach everyone to do as he does) is not to be judged by you: leave his judgement with God. After all, the prophets in olden times also acted in that way. (*Did.* 11.11)

Most attempts to explain this statement are based on noting, first, that there is a link between 'mystery', 'earthly' and 'church' which is reminiscent of what we find in Ephesians 5.22–33 where the relationship of husband and wife is seen as somehow being an image in this world of the relationship of Christ to the church which is said to be a 'profound mystery' (Eph. 5.32). Second, whatever these prophets are doing is like something that the prophets did in Israel, and this may refer to something like the marriage of Hosea to the prostitute Gomer and having children with her (Hos. 1—3). That marriage was intended to demonstrate in an earthly way the divine mystery of God's continuing love for his people even when they were unfaithful. So did early Christian prophets enter into marriages as demonstrations of the love of Christ for the new Israel? There have been as many theories as commentators. Some have seen this as ordinary marriages after which these prophets held that they had a right to support for both themselves and their wives (this would fit with Paul's obscure statement in 1 Cor. 9.5). Others have seen it as some sort of 'spiritual marriage' in the sense of a man travelling with a woman who is not his wife – which would have been seen as scandalous within their cultural world – but who remains his 'betrothed' (this would fit with Paul's advice, also obscure, on not marrying for anyone who does not need to marry 'but having his desire under control, and has determined this in his heart, to keep her as his betrothed, he will do well' [1 Cor 7.36–38 (rsv)]). Which is the more likely explanation? Probably the second, for the simple reason that it would throw some light on what Paul clearly thought was a practice in the communities with which he was in contact. Clearly, some in these communities were suspicious about the whole matter: well, they were to leave it to God's judgement. Meanwhile, we should remind ourselves, yet again, of the limits of our own knowledge of early Christian practices.

Other visitors

As we should expect, there were other Christians – not teachers, apostles or prophets – who were moving about the Roman Empire and who made themselves known to the communities they passed through on their journeys. So the *Didache* has guidance on how they also should be treated and what they should expect from their sisters and brothers in Christ. The same basic approach is taken towards these 'ordinary' Christian visitors as with visits from the apostles and prophets, which shows us that the communities were taking the position (also advocated by Matthew) that they were not to give special honours to the apostles and prophets but treat every Christian equally as a brother (Matt. 23.1–8).

> Now anyone coming in the Lord's name should be made welcome; then you can test him, using your own insight [into human nature] to see if he is genuine or a fraud.
>
> If the visitor is someone who is passing through, help him as much as you can. However, he is not to stay for more than two days – or three out of necessity.
>
> If the visitor wishes to settle in your community, then, if he is a craftsman, he should work for his living.
>
> But if he does not have a trade, then use your own judgement to decide how he is to live among you as a Christian: but he is not to live in idleness.
>
> If he is unhappy with this arrangement then he is a 'christ-monger'. Be on the watch for such people. (*Did.* 12)

Everyone who has been involved in running a charity knows this dilemma in one way or another. Welcome and support is something that Christians should give; but at the same time no one should be allowed to abuse that generosity and sponge rather than work. Such people are not brothers who should be welcomed in Christ as coming in the Lord's name but people who are using the name of Christian for their own ends. The name the *Didache* coins for such a sponger is *christemporos* (literally: one who trades on the name of Christ), which is sometimes rendered, as here, by the word 'christmonger'.

The community was based on all pulling together and sharing the task of welcome: so no individual was to live within a community and take advantage of it. The cases were to be decided as the community saw fit: in the case of someone with a skill, it was simple – they were to work; but it was to be left to the community's discretion in the case of those who had no trade to ply – but they were not to feel that they had to support someone who would not work.

These regulations help us to understand Paul's concerns about any implication that he was making a living out of the gospel (1 Cor. 9.1–18), but also to understand this instruction he gave to the Thessalonians:

> Now we command you, brethren, in the name of our Lord Jesus Christ, that you keep away from any brother who is living in idleness and not in accord with the tradition that you received from us. For you yourselves know how you ought to imitate us; we were not idle when we were with you, we did not eat any one's bread without paying, but with toil and labour we worked night and day, that we might not burden any of you. It was not because we have not that right, but to give you in our conduct an example to imitate. For even when we were with you, we gave you this command: If any one will not work, let him not eat. For we hear that some of you are living in idleness, mere busybodies, not doing any work. Now such

persons we command and exhort in the Lord Jesus Christ to do their work in quietness and to earn their own living.

(2 Thess. 3.6–12 [RSV])

The community was to be welcoming and generous, but they did not have to allow themselves to be used by those just looking for an idle life.

Supporting the prophets and teachers

Paul in 1 Corinthians 9.14 says that 'the Lord commanded that those who proclaim the gospel should get their living by the gospel' (RSV) even though he does not make use of that right himself. What that right meant in practice we see in this section of the *Didache*:

Any true prophet who wishes to settle down among you is worthy of his food. In the same way, any true teacher is like a labourer who is worthy of his food.

So take the first fruits of the vine and the harvest, of cattle and sheep, and present these first fruits to the prophets because they are, to you, the high priests.

But if you have no prophet [settled in your community], then give the first fruits to the poor.

When you bake a batch of bread, take the first loaf and present it as it says in the commandment.

Do likewise when you open a fresh flask of wine or oil: take the first portion from it and present it to the prophets.

So also with money and cloth and other commodities: set aside the first fruits, and give it – as much as seems right to you – according to the commandment. (*Did.* 13)

We have noticed in earlier chapters that the community of the *Didache* was very familiar with the normal practices of Judaism as laid out in the law of Moses. Perhaps nowhere is this closeness between the communities of the *Didache* and contemporary Jewish communities better seen than here (> Niederwimmer, 1998, pp. 192–3). The Christians are to keep up the practices of 'the first fruits' that were prescribed in the law as being offered to the Lord by way of support for the priestly tribe of Levi (> Draper, 2006b). The *Didache* says 'according to the commandment' and we must read this as meaning 'as lawfully commanded' for there was not one single commandment regarding 'the first fruits' but many scattered across the Scriptures. For instance, the rule about 'the first fruits' of wine/grapes is found in Numbers 13.20 and Deuteronomy 18.4; that about the harvest in Exodus 34.22; that about bread in Leviticus 23.17; and that about oil in Deuteronomy 18.4. Among the Jews this offering was a way both of honouring God for his goodness and of supporting the praise of God through supporting the priesthood. Now, in the *Didache*, it is carrying on these two functions: it praises God and supports the work of the prophets who seem to have inherited the rights of the 'high priests'.

When we read in Matthew that the labourer deserves his food (Matt. 10.10) – Luke says he deserves his wages (Luke 10.7) – we see that these labourers are the apostles, prophets and teachers: they are to be offered support as the Levites were offered support by being given a share in the food available. And, if there is no need to offer them support, then those first fruits are to be given to the poor.

This presentation of 'the first fruits' to these prophets and teachers as if they were the replacement for the 'high priests' appears to be inconsistent with the emphasis earlier in the *Didache* on the prophets and teachers not earning a living from their Christian service except for basic food while they are present in a church (*Did.* 11.3–6, 9, 12). However, this inconsistency shows that the *Didache* was a living document that was being adapted to circumstances as times changed. Such inconsistencies are an inherent part of most practical literature: one rule emerged in one situation, another when the situation changed, and no one noticed the lack of consistency. Textual consistency is something that belongs to works that emerge from the scholar's study or the lawyer's office: documents produced and amended in the course of the evolution of living communities rarely display such neatness.

'Bishops and deacons'

The apostles, prophets and teachers seem to have been mainly people who moved from place to place, working with one church after another. There are those who settle in a community – one cannot remain always on the move – but this seems to be the exception, for there are communities that do not have such people living with them and they are to use the 'first fruits' for the poor. By contrast, each community has to appoint people from among them to provide leadership and service in the community, and these are to come from within the community, live there, and be part of the church in that particular place.

> Select for yourselves bishops and deacons: men who are worthy of the Lord, humble, not greedy for money, honest, and well tested, because these too carry out for you the service of the prophets and teachers.
> Therefore, you should not despise them but treat them as your honoured men like the prophets and teachers. (*Did.* 15.1–2)

In some communities it appears that the men chosen to take the lead in the community were known as 'presbyters' (literally: elders) while in other communities they were called 'bishops and deacons'. In these latter communities 'the bishops' were not one group and 'the deacons' another, but rather the leaders were known by this double-barrelled designation to bring out the twin aspects of their task: to have a watchful eye over the community *and* to be its servants. So we could render 'bishops and deacons' as 'bishop-deacons'. There is no hint that there was as yet only one bishop, but rather in each church there were several men – there is no hint anywhere that women could perform this service – who were 'bishops and deacons'. Likewise, there is no hint that these 'bishops and deacons' were those who offered the blessing to the Father at the Eucharist or that they baptized new members.

It was only later, in the early decades of the second century, that this whole matter of leadership began to take on its more developed structures of a bishop, with presbyters, and then deacons (all arranged in a pyramidal structure of authority), and then still later emerged the notion that only bishops and presbyters could preside at the Eucharist with the deacons acting in an assisting capacity.

Other concerns

The *Didache* contains one final set of instructions relating to the interaction of people within a church:

> Now when you come to correct one another, this is to be done in a composed way, and not in anger, just as you find in the gospel.
> And when someone does wrong against his neighbour, let no one speak to him, indeed he is not to hear anything from you, until he repents.
> Now with regard to your prayers and almsgiving, indeed all your actions, do them all in the way that you find them prescribed in our Lord's gospel. (*Did.* 15.2–4)

We know from scattered references in later documents that Christians sought to offer correction to one another just as is mentioned here. The concern is that this correction should be a composed affair aimed at showing the Christian who had gone astray the right way, rather than becoming, as is so often the case when someone offers another 'correction', the occasion for 'tearing a strip off them' in angry denunciation. In every community there are going to be actions by others that irritate us, other actions that annoy us, and still others that 'drive us up the wall' because they seem so silly or wrong-headed – it is all too easy to offer angry 'corrections'! Indeed, this problem was so serious that there was not just this teaching on the subject, but the matter was included in the preaching of the good news. However, what form this teaching took in the *kerugma* is unknown to us; alas, none of the four preachers of the gospel whose Gospels we still have seems to have addressed it.

By contrast, we do have a Gospel setting for the teaching on prayer and almsgiving and other works of piety:

Beware of practising your piety before men in order to be seen by them; for then you will have no reward from your Father who is in heaven.

Thus, when you give alms, sound no trumpet before you, as the hypocrites do in the synagogues and in the streets, that they may be praised by men. Truly, I say to you, they have received their reward. But when you give alms, do not let your left hand know what your right hand is doing, so that your alms may be in secret; and your Father who sees in secret will reward you.

And when you pray, you must not be like the hypocrites; for they love to stand and pray in the synagogues and at the street corners, that they may be seen by men. Truly, I say to you, they have received their reward. But when you pray, go into your room and shut the door and pray to your Father who is in secret; and your Father who sees in secret will reward you.

(Matt. 6.1–6 [RSV])

What is laid out in the *Didache* as simple guidance takes on a larger context in story form in the preaching of Matthew. Here we have another indication that the communities that were inspired on hearing the narratives of the great preachers, the evangelists, were the same ones that were formed in discipleship by texts like the *Didache*.

Their concerns, our concerns

Some of the problems that so exercised the formulators of the *Didache* are unknown to modern Christians, and vice versa.

Some of the problems have remained constant in the churches. The benefit of reading this ancient text – and other ancient Christian texts – is that it shows us both similarities and differences. Those issues that are common are often the key issues of discipleship; those which are specific are very often secondary and derivative issues. There are some today who may wonder that there was so much concern about frauds and spongers – but this is what was their most pressing issue. Likewise, there are those who will wonder why I have not spent most of this chapter looking at the 'three-fold ministry' or the necessity for a duly ordained presbyter for a 'genuine' Eucharist because this is, today, their most pressing issue, but these were not even topics within the world of the *Didache*.

However, all those shifting concerns about structures might reveal a deeper truth about Christianity: it is a faith that makes demands within a real community and about how it lives in the world as it bears witness to the Christ. From this need flow all those structures that we as human beings need: they are but means to an end, and always somehow provisional relative to the end. From this also flows a warning: when concerns over structures become noisy and strident – the sort of thing that can cause Christians to split into hostile groups, as has happened all too often in our history – then we have confused means with ends.

7

Fears and hope

Following its parent Judaism of the Second Temple, Christianity views time as linear. There is a line running from a beginning up to now: this is all our history; and the line continues running through an ever-passing moment we label 'now' into the future. There, in front of us, lies our hope – and, also, the source of our fears. This linear view of time is so embedded within Western culture (it is not only part of the Christian inheritance but is at the heart of our physics as when we refer to 'The Big Bang') that we are apt to think that it is the only way to view time. But other and earlier cultures have thought of time in many other ways. The most common alternative is to think of time as a great circle: all recurs in cosmic cycles – and this view pops up in such notions as reincarnation and the 'migration of souls' or in astrology where events on earth are presented as explicable by the cycles of the heavens. For those who look on time as linear, the present is the outcome of the past, and the future is something that is open: it is being built, partly, by our decisions now.

For Israel and for us, this view of time underpins almost everything we say about God, the creation and our response to God. History began because God brought all into existence at the creation, and God made himself known in history and entered a covenant with his people. Over time this relationship grew, and God promised a time when he would establish a new relationship not just with his chosen people but with all his children. We see this notion of the future promised time in this oracle from Malachi (1.11), which is used in the

Didache (14.3), when a pure offering is what is presented to God:

> For from the rising of the sun to its setting my name is great among the nations, and in every place incense is offered to my name, and a pure offering; for my name is great among the nations, says the LORD of hosts. (Mal. 1.11 [RSV])

God began history, showed his hand in history, and, for the disciples of Jesus, this involvement reached a new level in Jesus: 'God with us' (Matt. 1.23). This view of history's promises being fulfilled in Jesus, the Anointed of the Father, was at the heart of the *kerugma*:

> the gospel of God, which he promised beforehand through his prophets in the holy scriptures, the gospel concerning his Son, who was descended from David according to the flesh and was declared to be Son of God with power according to the spirit of holiness by resurrection from the dead, Jesus Christ our Lord ... (Rom. 1.1–4 [NRSV])

The early Christians held that the Logos was at the beginning of history (John 1.1–3), had become flesh and dwelt among us (John 1.14), and would come again to take his people to himself (John 14.3). They even had a simple shorthand to express this: Jesus the Christ was 'the Alpha and the Omega, the beginning and the end' (Rev. 21.6 [RSV]) 'who is and who was and who is to come, the Almighty' (Rev. 1.8 [RSV]) – see Figure 7.1 opposite. The Christians were a people waiting in the aftermath of the Christ for him to return in glory 'to judge the living and the dead' (Acts 10.42; 2 Tim. 4.1). For all his followers, Jesus was ushering in the kingdom; the Day of the Lord had come; they were the new people of the final age of the world; and for the first generations it seemed that the time between Jesus' ascension to the Father and his coming again in glory was going to be only a short time. Paul expressed this view that the time of the Christ's return was at hand when he wrote:

I mean, brothers and sisters, the appointed time has grown short; from now on, let even those who have wives be as though they had none, and those who mourn as though they were not mourning, and those who rejoice as though they were not rejoicing, and those who buy as though they had no possessions, and those who deal with the world as though they had no dealings with it. For the present form of this world is passing away.

(1 Cor. 7.29–31 [NRSV])

Moreover, there was not just one view of the future, however short, but several. Jesus preached that the kingdom was at hand, but it was the kingdom of the Father's welcome. The new life of the disciples would open them into the welcome of the Father's forgiveness. In this view of the future, the Father's forgiveness is paramount, and we see it in the story of 'the prodigal son' (Luke 15.11–32) or Jesus' statement that the woman who anointed him had been forgiven much and therefore could love much: 'Therefore, I tell you, her sins, which were many, have

Figure 7.1 Chi-rho drawing
The Chi-rho (= 'Christ') set between an alpha and an omega: this was not simply a logo, but a succinct statement of the Christian view of history.

been forgiven; hence she has shown great love' (Luke 7.47
[NRSV]). However, there were also Christians who still looked
to the future with the more widely based notion – preached,
for example, by John the Baptist (e.g. Matt. 3.12) – that the
future would be one of a terrible trial when God would take
vengeance on sinners:

> See, the day is coming, burning like an oven, when all the
> arrogant and all evildoers will be stubble; the day that comes
> shall burn them up, says the LORD of hosts, so that it will leave
> them neither root nor branch.   (Mal. 4.1 [NRSV])

A still more frightening view of the future was that there was
going to be a massive time of trial when the forces of light and
the forces of darkness would join in battle; then, after a terrify-
ing cosmic struggle, God would be triumphant and he would
rescue those who were loyal to him. We refer to this strand of
viewing the future as 'apocalypticism' and it was a significant
force in Judaism in the time of Jesus. The most familiar examples
of this movement are in the book of Daniel, in the passages
in the Gospels such as Mark 13.5–37 (with parallels in Matt.
24.4–36 and Luke 21.8–36) which we label 'the synoptic
apocalypse', and in the book that is known variously as 'the
Apocalypse of John' or the 'book of Revelation'. Apocalypticism
is characterized by a select group being given a secret key to
understand the history that is about to occur, when a great
battle will take place (the first rumbling can already be heard
on the horizon), and then will come the final victory of God
(> Collins, 1984).

All these various positions on the future – would the return
of Jesus be soon or in the distance, would the final victory be
the banquet of forgiveness, a trial followed by retribution,
or a mighty battle of the men and angels against Satan and
darkness – can be found intermingled to a greater or lesser
extent in the writings of the first generations of Christians.
A more-or-less consistent view of the final times would only

emerge in the second century; and even after that time the old patterns of apocalyptic thought would continue to pop up in times of fear, and they are still today a feature of some branches of Christianity (> Cohn, 1970). Only when we are aware of these various, and intermingled, positions about the future can we appreciate what the *Didache* says about how Christians should look forward.

Be prepared!

The *Didache*'s teaching about the future takes the form of a little homily. It still has the tone of instructions being given as commands, but the sense of regulations is absent. While reading through this homily you will notice the number of times that it seems to echo verses from across the writings in the canonical collection – now an echo of Paul, then a echo of a parable from one of the Gospels, then something from somewhere else – but always with a slightly different tone or nuance. We have to think of all the hopes and fears of those Christian communities as forming a common imagination: each text is a particular expression, each is distinct, and yet each helps us appreciate all the others.

> Watch over your lives. You must not let your lamps go out, nor should you let your loins be ungirded, rather you should be ready because you do not know the hour at which our Lord is coming.
> Gather together frequently and seek those things that are good for your souls. Otherwise what use will having faith over all the time of your life be to you, if at the end of time you are not made perfect. (*Did.* 16.1–2)

The lamp – usually a simple affair made of clay burning olive oil – was already a well-used metaphor for faith by the time of Jesus: the Lord was a lamp for life that dispelled darkness (Ps. 18.28), and like a lamp for one's way (Ps. 119.105), but it was also a symbol of someone who was ready, prepared and had planned for the future – and who could cope with the unexpected. Hence the use made of the image of lamps in the parable of the wise and foolish girls in Matthew 25. The wise were ready for the arrival of the bridegroom at an unexpected hour. But here in the *Didache* the symbol of the lamp is made even more explicit: the lamp is a symbol of anyone who is watching and waiting for the Lord.

We hear this opening sentence in different places in the preaching of the evangelists. Mark has:

> Heaven and earth will pass away, but my words will not pass away.
>
> But of that day or that hour no one knows, not even the angels in heaven, nor the Son, but only the Father. Take heed, watch; for you do not know when the time will come. It is like a man going on a journey, when he leaves home and puts his servants in charge, each with his work, and commands the doorkeeper to be on the watch. Watch therefore – for you do not know when the master of the house will come, in the evening, or at midnight, or at cockcrow, or in the morning – lest he come suddenly and find you asleep. And what I say to you I say to all: Watch. (Mark 13.31–37 [rsv])

And Matthew (24.42–44) also has the command to watch for the Lord is coming at an unexpected hour. While Luke has a slightly different approach to this notion of being ready with one's lamp burning when the Lord says:

> Let your loins be girded and your lamps burning
> . . .
> You also must be ready; for the Son of man is coming at an unexpected hour. (Luke 12.35 and 40 [rsv])

The *Didache* expresses common teaching and then adds that while the community waits it should assemble frequently because this is a way of keeping their attention fixed on what is important in following the Way or, to put it metaphorically, to keep their lamps burning brightly.

A time of tribulation

A very common theme in early Christianity was a fear about a time before 'the last days' when society will break down, loyalties will evaporate, good people will turn nasty, and corruption will enter the assembly of God. Here is how this fear of the future expresses itself in the *Didache*:

> For in the last days there are going to be many false prophets and those who would corrupt you, then the sheep will turn into wolves, and love will turn into hate.
> Then when lawlessness is increasing, people will hate and persecute and be treacherous with one another. Then, indeed, the Deceiver of this world will appear as if a son of God and he will do signs and wonders and the earth will be delivered into his hands and he will commit lawless acts such as have never been seen since the world began.
> Then all people will be brought through the trial of fire.
> Then many will fall away and will perish; but those who stand firm in their faith will be saved by the Cursed One himself.
>
> (*Did.* 16.3–5)

These few lines are almost a summary of early Christian apocalypticism. Compare this passage with the following statements from around the time of the *Didache* (you will notice that the same motifs crop up again and again but in different combinations).

That false prophets will arise and corrupt Christians: 'False messiahs and false prophets will appear and produce signs and omens, to lead astray, if possible, the elect. But be alert; I have already told you everything' (Mark 13.22–23 [NRSV]); this statement by Mark is followed exactly by Matthew (24.24–25) and in yet another form in Matthew 24.4–5. The image of the sheep become wolves also appears, but in a different way in Matthew's preaching: 'Beware of false prophets, who come to you in sheep's clothing but inwardly are ravenous wolves' (7.15 [NRSV]). And the idea that all this will be in the last days is found in this statement: 'First of all you must understand this, that in the last days scoffers will come, scoffing and indulging their own lusts' (2 Pet. 3.3 [NRSV]).

That this final time will be one of lawlessness and treachery, when the Christians will be hated, appears in two forms, one in Mark and the other in Matthew:

Brother will betray brother to death, and a father his child, and children will rise against parents and have them put to death; and you will be hated by all because of my name. But the one who endures to the end will be saved.

But when you see the desolating sacrilege set up where it ought not to be (let the reader understand), then those in Judea must flee to the mountains; someone on the housetop must not go down or enter the house to take anything away; someone in the field must not turn back to get a coat.

(Mark 13.12–16 [NRSV])

And in this form:

Then they will hand you over to be tortured and will put you to death, and you will be hated by all nations because of my name. Then many will fall away, and they will betray one another and hate one another. And many false prophets will arise and lead many astray. And because of the increase of lawlessness, the love of many will grow cold. But anyone who endures to the end will be saved. (Matt. 24.9–13 [NRSV])

The imagery was swirling around the early churches combining and recombining to make different points. This variety should serve to remind us that we have to read all these texts, the *Didache* and the Gospels, primarily as a witness to the mindset of the early Christianity as it struggled to make sense of its beliefs in what it saw as a potentially hostile environment, while at the same time coping with the fact that its expectations were, day by day, changing because the Christ had not yet returned.

In this time of trial the Christians are not just opposing wicked human beings who hate them and want to persecute them, but are imagined confronting a supernatural enemy. This enemy has many names (most commonly the enemy is called 'Satan') but in the *Didache* it is simply referred to as 'the Deceiver'. This name, and this activity of deceiving the Christians, is also found in a letter attributed to John the Evangelist:

> Many deceivers have gone out into the world, those who do not confess that Jesus Christ has come in the flesh; any such person is the deceiver and the antichrist! Be on your guard, so that you do not lose what we have worked for, but may receive a full reward. (2 John 7–8 [NRSV])

And the Deceiver will be able to do many mighty deeds, a notion we find in an early letter of Paul:

> The coming of the lawless one is apparent in the working of Satan, who uses all power, signs, lying wonders, and every kind of wicked deception for those who are perishing, because they refused to love the truth and so be saved.
> (2 Thess. 2.9–10 [NRSV])

This time will be one of fiery trial:

> Beloved, do not be surprised at the fiery ordeal that is taking place among you to test you, as though something strange were happening to you. But rejoice in so far as you are sharing Christ's sufferings, so that you may also be glad and shout for joy when his glory is revealed. (1 Pet. 4.12–13 [NRSV])

But, as we have seen in statements just quoted (Mark 13.12–16; Matt. 10.21–22 and 24.9–13), they believed that those who endure will be saved. Indeed, if they stand firm in faith (see 1 Pet. 5.9), they will be saved by 'the Cursed One himself'. This seems to our ears a very strange title for the Christ, but it was used among the first generation of Christians – but then, probably because the idea of describing the Lord as 'the Cursed One', no matter how understood, seemed too inappropriate it disappeared completely. Paul once refers to the Christ in this way: 'Christ redeemed us from the curse of the law by becoming a curse for us – for it is written, "Cursed is everyone who hangs on a tree"' (Gal. 3.13 [NRSV]). The title is a way of referring to Jesus on the cross by reference to this statement in the law:

> When someone is convicted of a crime punishable by death and is executed, and you hang him on a tree, his corpse must not remain all night upon the tree; you shall bury him that same day, for anyone hung on a tree is under God's curse.
>
> (Deut. 21.22–23 [NRSV])

For those who referred to Jesus as 'the Cursed One' it was a reference to the shameful nature of his death, and shows us that they understood that death as Jesus removing the sins of his followers by taking their 'curse' upon himself. The implications of the use of the title, the Cursed One, in the *Didache* is that by undergoing the cross Jesus saved his people: his people are saved by what he himself did which caused him to be called 'the Cursed One'.

Not only does this passage in the *Didache* show us the fears of the communities about the end of the world but also the overlaps show how the *Didache* reflects 'the common knowledge' about this belief among the first generations of disciples.

Christ in glory

While apocalyptic fear, as we have just seen, was an important feature of the life of early Christian communities, the fundamental 'gospel' – the good news announced – was that the Christ had triumphed. He had fought his dual with death, and risen triumphantly: his tomb was empty, and so the Christians could await that day when he would return in glory and they too would then leave their tombs; 'for the hour is coming when all who are in the tombs will hear his voice and come forth, those who have done good, to the resurrection of life, and those who have done evil, to the resurrection of judgment' (John 5.28–29 [RSV]). So if the *Didache* ended with apocalyptic fear,

it would seem out of step with the hope of those early communities – indeed, if the *Didache* were out of step with that
hope, one would wonder how widely it was used in training
new disciples within communities. However, the *Didache* ends
with the 'signs' of the Christ's final victory. The imagery of this
victory belongs to the apocalyptic imagination (> Rowland,
1982), but there is an important difference. Instead of ringing
out with the fearsome judgement of God annihilating the
wicked, it presents a vision of the Lord coming in glory with
all his people: the saints. Here is how the *Didache* ends:

And then, the signs of the truth will appear:
The first sign will be the heavens opening;
Then [second,] the sound of the trumpet;
And, third, the resurrection of the dead –
but not of everyone, but as it has been said: 'the Lord will come
and all his saints with him'.
Then the world will see the Lord coming upon the clouds of
heaven.   (*Did.* 16.6–8)

The whole passage, and especially the notion of signs ap-
pearing in heaven, is expressed in this passage of Matthew
(> Verheyden, 2005):

Then the sign of the Son of man will appear in heaven, and
then all the tribes of the earth will mourn, and they will see
"the Son of man coming on the clouds of heaven" with power
and great glory. And he will send out his angels with a loud
trumpet call, and they will gather his elect from the four
winds, from one end of heaven to the other.

(Matt. 24.30–31 [NRSV])

Here the trumpet is like that used by an army to call soldiers
to rally round, but by the time Matthew preached this image
of the final trumpet was already well established, and in the
Didache we see it used in a less developed way. For Paul,
writing to the Thessalonians, the trumpet was a call to the dead
to wake up for they would now arise to a heavenly life: 'For the

Lord himself, with a cry of command, with the archangel's call and with the sound of God's trumpet, will descend from heaven, and the dead in Christ will rise first' (1 Thess. 4.16 [NRSV]). But later, writing to the Corinthians, the trumpet is far more like the signal that the end, and with that the final victory of Christ, has come:

> Listen, I will tell you a mystery! We will not all die, but we will all be changed, in a moment, in the twinkling of an eye, at the last trumpet. For the trumpet will sound, and the dead will be raised imperishable, and we will be changed. For this perishable body must put on imperishability, and this mortal body must put on immortality.　　　　(1 Cor. 15.51–53 [NRSV])

This reference in 1 Corinthians expresses a notion of the trumpet as a sign that is perhaps closer to that in the *Didache*, and, as in the *Didache*, the trumpet is just before the resurrection.

Then, finally, the Lord will return on the clouds 'with all his saints with him'. The text referred to in the *Didache* when it says 'as it has been said' is a prophecy from the prophet Zechariah:

> And the valley of my mountains shall be stopped up, for the valley of the mountains shall touch the side of it; and you shall flee as you fled from the earthquake in the days of Uzziah king of Judah. Then the LORD your God will come, and all the holy ones with him.　　　　(14.5 [RSV])

This was one of those verses of the Scriptures that were in frequent use among the first Christians to help them explain why they were placing their hope in Jesus. We see Paul allude to that same prophecy in this statement:

> may the Lord make you increase and abound in love to one another and to all men, as we do to you, so that he may establish your hearts unblamable in holiness before our God and Father, at the coming of our Lord Jesus with all his saints.
>
> 　　　　(1 Thess. 3.12–13 [RSV])

In just three sentences the *Didache* sums up Christian hope and expresses the common view of the Christians of that time about where this will all end. The communities of the saints will be gathered, finally, with their Lord, triumphant over all.

It has been suggested that the *Didache* may once have had a longer ending (> Aldridge, 1999), but there is a certain crispness to the ending as we have it that makes the notion of a longer ending unnecessary. So rather than speculate about what it 'might have had' it is better, all in all, to take the text just as we have it.

Why this apocalypticism?

While today there is a strong strand of apocalypticism among Christians, usually looking back to the same texts in the New Testament with which the *Didache* overlaps, this is not the mainstream, and most Christians see those who preach 'the end is nigh' and can explain current affairs in terms of the beginning of 'the tribulation' as eccentric. So how do we account for it being so widely found in early Christian communities? No complete explanation is possible, but it is worth bearing these factors in mind.

First, apocalypticism in Judaism seems to have arisen out of the role that prophecy played within the religion of the time of the Second Temple. These were promises by God, and so they should come to fulfilment. This interest in the final fulfilment, when God would bring his justice into the world, was widespread across many forms of Judaism and, not surprisingly, it played an important part within those movements which saw themselves as being the new Judaism, distinct from the lukewarm 'ordinary' Judaism around them. So not only was it in the religious air all Jews in Palestine were breathing, but it would have been attractive to the very people who would have been willing to listen to John the Baptist or Jesus.

Second, the followers of Jesus took as a starting point of their faith that prophecy had just been fulfilled, that God had intervened in history showing his hand, in Jesus. So if God had just intervened, then all that was expected about the end times might now be in train. Apocalypticism is a way of understanding current events within a great historical plan. Now they believed that Jesus had explained history to them, and so all that was expected would soon come about. Jesus had risen and departed from them, but had promised he would return and take them to where he was going: so maybe it would all happen in a matter of years or decades (> Yarbro Collins, 1984). Certainly Paul, in the early years of his preaching, thought that the Return of the Christ would not be too far in the future. Only with the passing of time would this Return become something that had to be understood in terms apart from the historical order of the creation.

Third, apocalyptic ways of looking at human affairs usually appear in societies that are under great stress. They sense that they are in a time of crisis, they are excluded from the power structures of the society, and often have a sense of being the righteous few suffering persecution from the sinful many. Such people seem to have been attracted to Christianity, and certainly the *Didache* shows us a people who believe they do not want to be linked with the proud, the arrogant or the mighty. They perceive themselves to be the poor, the oppressed, the righteous few, and to be a people who suffer at the hands of the wicked. It shows us communities with many of the classic signs of being stressed and alienated, and who still want to explain how it happens that God lets good people suffer.

This apocalyptic section points out that when Christians look back to their early roots, they cannot simply engage in a simple act of repetition nor either adopt or reject positions *en bloc*. Just as the *Didache* emerged out of a community's reflection on its faith and its situation, so the work of theology must continue in the community. Theology is part of a community's very life, rather than some rarefied activity of religious boffins or the handed-down 'answers' of religious leaders.

The end of the road

One of the little stylistic features of many ancient texts is that if they are dealing with a process, a sequence of events leading from *a* to *b* to *c* . . . , then that process is reflected in the very sequence of what we find in the text. The beginning is at the beginning and the end is at the end! Despite its brevity, the pattern can be seen in the *Didache*. It opens with a choice facing every individual: the choice of life as a disciple of the Lord or death; it ends with all the disciples being gathered into eternal life by the Lord.

The pattern within the text is not rigid – oral texts never have that neat logic of texts produced for private reading and for study as a book – but it is clearly there, with each step marked by words indicating that it is now time to move on to the next topic (> Varner, 2008, p. 310). Having now gone through the text we can summarize it by looking at the step-by-step plan. The *Didache* opens with an encounter with an individual outside the Church. That person has been brought to that point by the preparation of the Spirit and an encounter with the Christians and their message. So the first step is to decide to set out on the Way, to hear its demands and learn what the Way demands from those who follow it and look to its promise of Life (> ch. 2 above). The next step is to join the community of the Christ through baptism which marks the boundary of the new people (> ch. 3 above). Then having entered the community, one had to learn its basic ways and times, its rules for regular fasting and prayer (> ch. 4 above); and then how to appreciate, indeed offer, the blessing, as the central meal which models discipleship and maintains the community in its most visible expression (> ch. 5 above). Then, knowing and living within that community as it, as a people, follows the Way, there was need for knowledge about how the community related to other Christians and needs for leaders (> ch. 6). Finally, the community looked to its future, its fears for the time of fiery trial it would have to face, and on to the final destination of the Way and the gathering of the community by the Lord: 'Then the world will see the Lord coming upon the clouds of heaven' (*Did.* 16.8).

8

The challenge of the *Didache*

This book has attempted to introduce an early Christian training guide to ways of being a disciple of Jesus. We have seen how it focuses on the community and its activities, stands alongside the community's great story, and gives us – in our very different world – a glimpse into what it meant to be a disciple of Jesus, to believe that he was the Father's child, the Anointed, and the teacher who had shown them the Way, and who would gather them at his return to himself. To examine these issues anew is, in itself, an important part of being a Christian. This is especially true when the lens we use is a text that is less familiar to us than those in the canonical collection, and therefore a text that can grab our attention by showing us what we thought we knew from a very different angle. But are there any aspects of our discipleship that the *Didache* challenges us in a particular way to examine afresh? The answer to the question must remain open: it depends on the whole variety of situations where Christians find themselves, their ways of understanding discipleship, and the problems they face. Each person who reflects on the *Didache* needs to draw up her/his own list, and that list will reflect their own experience of being part of a church, their views about the Church, its books, and how discipleship relates to individual action.

However, it is easy to produce a wish list in this form: it was great back then, so let us imitate it! But while it is possible to imitate specific items we see elsewhere – and Christians are always borrowing from one another, from the past and from elsewhere – the task of trying to become more self-aware by comparing ourselves to the past is far more difficult. This is the attempt to become aware of the tacit assumptions of our own times, our inbuilt biases and our systemic misrepresentations of Christian discipleship. Here the focus is not on the bits in the past that we find interesting or charming, but on how we can learn more about ourselves by looking at relatives, but very foreign relatives.

The most common attitude to the past – and the one adopted very frequently in preaching that is based on the canonical collection – is to see something which is jarring between then and now. Then there is the assumption that the position *then* is the norm, and we should adopt it now! This is like walking through a museum and making a list of the items you might want to take home with you. However, learning *from* the past is not the same as imitating it. It is a process of comparison that involves looking at how various elements fitted together in the past and seeing whether or not those elements fit together today. This is more like visiting a very foreign country and being struck by how different it all is: things we 'take for granted' are problematic for them, but what is a 'big deal' for us is seen as unworthy of comment over there. At the end of the process, we should know more about ourselves, more about the other, and have new goals for ourselves inspired by the other, but not simply adopted from them. Like the traveller returning from the foreign country we want to have new ideas for what we can do differently having gained new self-knowledge, not simply some curios that we put on the mantelpiece.

A central tenet of any such comparison is that we move beyond some of the very simple analogies of history that we commonly use. Take, for example, this analogy: 'the mighty oak has grown from the tiny acorn' – and we look on the past as the acorn and the present as the oak. However, from acorn to oak is a matter of genetic programming: only an acorn can lie behind an oak, and an acorn cannot produce a sycamore or fir tree! However, human affairs are not so predictable: there is the continuity between now and back then, but there are ups and downs as well! We cannot make the assumption that the present is the inevitable outcome of the past: people get things wrong, sometimes other things intervene, sometimes there are unexpected blessings and sometimes there are unwelcome accidents. One culture received a religion in one way, another in a different way, and some virtually reinvented Christianity when it arrived among them. We can see these processes today, and they were also operative in the past. Comparison does not make one period, then or now, normative, but assumes that learning from comparison is a way of becoming more self-knowing as disciples. There is a tendency to see the past as a 'golden age' and use terms like 'in New Testament times' (*sotto voce*: 'all was lovely and pure then'), and then think that it can be just reinvented. Likewise, we tend to decide that our views, our practices, or our doctrines are not only true, but the only possible genuine Christian position, and we use terms like 'authentic' or 'orthodox' (*sotto voce*: 'people who are not with us are wrong') and then we only look back and see the bits that fit with our positions, and simply ignore the rest! In the first case we reinvent the past to image the future we would like, in the second case we reinvent the past to image the present we do like. So if 'oaks come from acorns' allows us to recognize continuities (and hence comparisons are meaningful) then it should be balanced by this, the opening line from L. P. Hartley's 1953 novel, *The Go-Between*: 'The past is a foreign country: they do things differently there'. Historical comparison may sometimes condemn the present or the past, but most times it should give us understanding for the task of acting in theologically aware ways now.

Because the *Didache* covers such a range of Christian life, there are any number of areas where we could make such comparisons between the life of discipleship then and now. However, I am going to take three topics and make *my* comparison, with the intention of showing the method of comparison rather than drawing out any particular points about the present where we might need to become more aware.

Morality, law and love

A common theme in Christianity since the time of the *Didache* until now is that of moral action: individuals are faced with choices and must choose between alternatives. This leaves us with two questions: first, how this aspect of discipleship is presented; and, second, how those demands were seen to possess a moral quality.

When Christians approach morality they usually do so using a few very well-trodden routes. The simplest is that there are certain actions that make one sinful, and the sinful person cannot exist in the presence of God. Here the core concern is not with the rightness/wrongness of an action, or its impact on others, but on the fact that it makes one a sinner, and if that happens then the need is for purification, individual for-giveness by God and the knowledge that one is now 'one of the saints' once more. It is a notion that is very close to the notions of ritual purity that one finds in Leviticus and Numbers, and so, not surprisingly, it will pay great attention to issues of personal sexual morality. The approach can be spotted in that the concern, after a sexual sin, is not with whether or not the action has victims but that the actor is now in a state of sin. The need for 'the sinner' is for some ritual – though many would object to this word – that allows that sinner to become 'justified' or 'forgiven'. The ritual might be 'Confession' for a Catholic or an intense moment of becoming aware of divine forgiveness and being 'personally saved by the Lord Jesus', for an Evangelical. But in either case, the most important aspect for the individual is that he/she is now 'OK' with God. Phew!

A second approach is that of doctrinaire morality: Christianity knows, as a religion, what is right and wrong, and making sure that people know this is a basic part of the message. So the acts that are right or wrong are laid down in a law – summarized in the Ten Commandments – and these are promulgated: follow them and you will be all right, fail to follow them and there is chaos in this world and the next. In this system there is great emphasis on morality as knowing what is right and wrong. There is a body of information about God, and part of this is knowing what he has legislated regarding conduct: it is a complete package, and there are great benefits for anyone who accepts the doctrine and what it teaches about conduct. In this approach, there is a similarity between the ways one views belonging to a civil society with its clear laws and the religious dimension of that society whose morality frequently can be closely mapped onto society's laws. This has been a dominant approach for much of Christian history where 'Church and State' operated in tandem, but it is far wider in its spread than Christianity, and the religious leaders saw themselves as a religious government or the religious wing of government: just as the sheriff patrolled some laws, the clerics kept an eye on other laws. God's law and society's regulations were linked, and religious leaders saw no difficulty in promoting both together, especially if the specifically religious demands were enshrined in secular law.

The third approach is to see morality as having its main themes, such as justice, originate in parallel to any particular religious code, and here the emphasis is upon how certain basic moral demands are far wider than any one religion. Then the religion recognizes that right action is part of the human response to the divine, and so adopts the ethics that are seen as a shared human inheritance as one of the elements of its religious adherence. So the demands of morality can be seen to arise out of the nature of creation or of the human condition and upright reflection on this situation, and then the business of following that 'wise path' is seen as part of the respect for the divine, or, in Christian terms, an aspect of discipleship. This approach has a long history in Christianity where it manifests

149

itself in such ethical forms as 'the natural law tradition' and the notion that right moral action and right human action are closely related.

The fourth approach is to take what we say about the divine nature and make it the basis for how we act: God is love, and therefore we come into existence through God's love; and we respond to God, and who we are, by seeking to act as loving beings. Augustine expressed this pithily when he said: 'Love, and then what you desire, do' (*Tractates on the First Letter of John* 7.4.8). In its more common form, all the particular rules and regulations of a religion are seen as expressions of a more basic understanding that flows from the very core of the religion. So the covenant between God and his people is the fundamental relationship that constitutes society, and all rules, ritual and ethical, give it concrete expression. In Jesus we see love become a human being, so the basis for his followers to act as human beings is to act with love.

These approaches, a morality of ritual purity, of doctrinaire moralism, of natural law, and a covenantal morality, are not mutually exclusive, and in every actual teaching system, religious culture and each Christian making choices there is a varying mix of these approaches. The question to pose to the *Didache* is what mix of approaches is found in it; and are any of them given priority? One very interesting point to observe is that despite its function as a basic training for apprentice Christians it presents the notion of a covenantal morality at its outset. Christians are not offered a choice between either right/wrong, or between being saved/damned, but between a way of life and a way of death, and the demands of the way of life flow from the need to love God and neighbour. Most modern 'simple' introductions to religion start with a moralism of 'what is right and wrong' and see the notions of a morality of love as belonging to a higher 'way of perfection': for ordinary people there are 'the commandments' and then for the few, 'the counsels'. Much Christian effort down the centuries has been devoted to a notion of moral purity, and even greater detail focused on sexual morality, whereas in the *Didache*, while this aspect of morality is not ignored, it is treated in a few general prescriptions on the major crimes. The *Didache* does appreciate the notion of ritual purity, as in its statements about fasting before baptism, but this – and its ritual regulations on fasting and prayer – is presented as part of the need for the community to cohere and form a new people. So the action of comparison is not to decide that '*Didache* good, moderns bad' (or vice versa), but to see how basic approaches vary between groups of Christians in various times and places, and to use this comparison to get a deeper insight into both the past and ourselves. So, having examined the *Didache*, what sort of training for new disciples would you, and your community, produce? And, just as importantly, why would you go down that particular route?

Historical comparison does not produce answers for what we should do today, but information that helps shape better questions about today and tomorrow. People who look to the past for answers to reuse today ignore the reality of human history with its variety; likewise people who do not consider the past when asking questions about today ignore the reality of human history with its continuities. Both camps who ignore history, though frequently at odds, are similar in approach in their confidence that 'answers' can be got easily.

The Christian meal

For most Christians today the most striking difference between modern practice and that mentioned in the *Didache* concerns what is now called the Eucharist (though many, demonstrating how we love the familiar in religion, prefer their denominational terms, most of which derive from far more recent times). From being the meal which bonded Christians it has become the battleground where all sorts of conflicts are fought out.

Sometimes these are doctrinal (as between differing denominations about whether you may or may not 'receive' at our Eucharist – or whether your Eucharist is even 'real'), sometimes these concern styles of practice or attitudes within groups (each has a Eucharist for its taste), and sometimes it is even used as a way of expressing approval or disapproval of individuals (for instance, can a gay person 'receive communion' or not?). The meals of Jesus were the means to train the disciples in his revolutionary model of the kingdom, but all too often our 'meals' are used as a litmus test to make sure boundaries are clear. What is most obvious at the practical level is that a meal ritual has become a ritual meal. The emphasis has shifted from blessing the Father – which is identical in early practice to 'offering thanks' – to an interest in what it is that is eaten, 'received', while 'the sacrifice of praise' that the *Didache* sees as inherent in the act of blessing the Father has become a series of questions about how this sacrifice is or is not identical with the death of Jesus on the cross, that death understood as a 'sacrifice'. So not only has actual practice changed (what happens at the gathering) but the purpose of the practice (from unifying the group to identifying those 'fully in communion' with the group), and also the perception of what is important and how that is best explained in relation to other aspects of Christian belief.

Again, it is easy to see the situation then as 'uncorrupted' and want to ignore what has happened since; and, likewise, it is easy to dismiss this as primitive and see the present as 'the fully developed photograph' when all is clear. Both positions will have their followers, but there is an even more complex kind of comparison that can be made that may promote greater understanding of what your group of Christians do, and help you to see good aspects of others' practice.

This comparison is based on seeking to see how and why the ritual evolved the way it did. All still have a gathering, someone to offer the prayer of blessing to the Father in words, a table, a loaf (of some shape, sort or form), a cup, and eating and drinking. Now each of these elements can be examined and questioned as to why the practice that is there arose in this form and whether or not it must be that way or can be otherwise.

Gathering

For some it is a rare event to gather for this meal, while for others it is weekly, and others it is a daily event: why is that the case? Is it a 'meal' with a liturgy of readings used as an introduction or is it really a readings/prayer service with the 'meal' tacked on? Are you even happy that it should be described as a 'meal'? Some Christians have the actual gathering broken into two spaces and separated by a wall, called an 'iconostasis', while others have rails between the clergy and the people. What signals do such divisions in the group send out to all concerned? Are these appropriate to the meal of Jesus and, whether they are or are not, would you be prepared to see changes in these practices?

If the meal gathering is not important, how did the community of the *Didache* get the matter so wrong that they invested such energy in it? And what importance is signalled to us by the way we organize our actual gathering?

Leader

In the *Didache* the task of leading the prayer of thanksgiving follows on from the fact that the church has gathered for the meal. But for many Christians today, one can only have the meal if one has a specially commissioned (and trained) person, a presbyter/priest, present; the meal follows from leadership. For other Christians the idea that only a specially ordained person can lead prayer is itself unnecessary. In each case there are many hidden assumptions not only about the nature of the meal but also about leadership, the Church and the action of the Spirit among the disciples of Jesus.

Table

The actual object on which the food is laid at the Eucharist is a table. It is a table because it was originally a real meal and these are eaten from tables, and because Jesus used the language of meals, tables and banquets. Moreover, we have descriptions of the altar in Jerusalem and it is nothing like that, and every museum with Roman artefacts has at least one ancient Mediterranean basic-style altar, essentially a short pillar, and nothing like it has ever been used in Christian practice. However, for many Christians, it is not thought of as a table but an 'altar', while for other Christians it may be 'the holy table' but it is never 'an altar'. So what does it mean to refer to the table as an altar, why does this occur, and would it be more appropriate to refer to it with a phrase like 'our table at the Eucharist is, for us, our altar'?

This is further complicated in that many traditions of Christians use a language of 'the table' and a language of 'the altar': what benefits flow from such rich use of language, and what are the disadvantages? What, indeed, should one see, and then name as an object, when one enters the space where Christians gather? In recent decades when many denominations have sought to redesign their church buildings to have a liturgy more sensitive to the notion of the Eucharist as a meal, warfare has ensued in the church over shapes and positions of this table, but, sadly, the debate has usually been dominated by aesthetics or nostalgia: looking back at how forms have evolved, what they have evolved from, why they evolved in the way they did, and asking whether or not they are in harmony with the original ideas would not only save much unseemly bickering, but make the whole process of change a positive one of making all concerned more aware of what they are doing.

Loaf

It might not seem important to mention the actual object that was eaten after the blessing of the Father at the Eucharist:

surely bread is simply bread? But it is worth noting that this practical question – quite apart from theological issues – has caused more than one schism in the history of Christianity. Sometime in the ninth century the Western churches, for practical reasons, began using unleavened loaves, and this put them at odds with the Easterners who rejected the idea that the meal of the living One could be celebrated with 'dead' bread. The West replied that it was originally a Passover, and so only unleavened bread should be used! In the early centuries the emphasis was on a unity, a loaf, divided into shares so that each could be part of the one loaf (> 1 Cor. 10). Later the emphasis shifted to the question of what it is that one eats. If the answer is 'the body of Christ', then the immediate response is to say that one cannot 'receive' it too often because one is unworthy! So eventually, only the leader ate at the Eucharist, so special little wafers, now of unleavened bread, became the norm. Instead of each having a share in a common loaf, each had an individual wafer on the occasions when one actually ate anything – as distinct from being simply present. No one seemed to notice that it is slightly absurd to imagine one can participate in a meal while not eating or drinking!

So what actual practice do you see in your community, and what does that indicate about your church's understanding, and the route it has taken to get to today? Is it a highway without junctions, or have there been many junctions so that the group could have arrived at many other destinations than where you are now? In fact, when we look back we always tend to see a straight road leading from the most remote past down to this very morning; but historical questioning reveals that routes that are straight in hindsight – history is written from the perspective of what actually evolved – are actually full of junctions and turns. We need only reflect that there were junctions in the past in order to recognize that there are choices facing us today. Looking then at the *Didache*'s image of a shared, broken loaf now becomes an inspiration for tomorrow.

Cup

One of the most shocking aspects of Jesus' meal practice with the disciples was that he invited them to share a cup: practically it demonstrated their intimacy and metaphorically it became an indication of the willingness to share in his life and destiny (> Mark 10.38). While sharing a loaf or a cake is a common demonstration of intimate sharing at table (just note how everyone at a birthday party has to have a piece of 'the birthday cake'), the notion of sharing a cup is counter-cultural: everyone wants their own glass, cup, drinking vessel – even if it is just made of paper. In the action of sharing a cup, drinking from one vessel one after another, we have an actual action that goes back to Jesus. In the *Didache* we find a prayer that expresses this action as part of our discipleship; while Paul in 1 Corinthians 11.25–28 sees this action as reflecting the intimacy of the new bonds between Christians and Christ. Indeed, it was this action of drinking that was emphasized, rather than what was drunk (wine was used, but also water), as being the imitation of the Christ. Yet, down the centuries it has always been an embarrassment to the churches who have found excellent reasons – and subsequently elegant theologies – to justify not doing it! Avoiding the actual action has taken the form of spoons, straws, moistening a wafer, many tiny cups, or simply declaring that it was enough for the priest to drink from the cup! But the underlying theme is clear: these communities faced with an aspect of Jesus' behaviour that upset them too much found ways to ignore it! It is a salutary lesson from the past: just because a group believes it is 'the Church' does not mean that it might not have forgotten important aspects of discipleship. So, recalling earlier practices and understandings, are we happy with what we have forgotten, or are there things to be recalled, restored, reinstalled into our practice? These are the questions that looking at the *Didache* can help us confront.

Eating and drinking

Sometime in the second century the meal of the Christians took on a far more formal aspect and it came to be known simply as 'the Eucharist' and the larger meal disappeared. Why this development took place is unclear. Most probably it was because the social disruption of slaves eating next to masters, poor with rich, and various ethnic differences all seemed too much. So the simplest thing was to share the Lord's loaf and cup, and skip further awkward table mixing! Yet human beings continued to be human beings, and eating together – but in exclusive gatherings – is part and parcel of being human, and every human meal has its own inbuilt ritual and subconscious statements. To gather and eat together expresses solidarity, it binds people, it expresses common purpose, it seals friendships, it expresses common joys and sorrows, it cements families, and it makes us sharing, speaking, sisters and brothers. Can you imagine any big event without a meal of some sort? Would you want to imagine life where we always eat alone or in silence!

Curiously, now that the Eucharist is usually a token rather than a real meal, and for some churches it is a peripheral event, the instinct to eat together is still there! When a new minister arrives and wants to 'build a sense of community' often the first suggestion will be having coffee and biscuits after the service. An evangelization programme may not have any mention of the Eucharist in its formal programme, but will have a meal included in the 'group activities' with everyone bringing some of the food to be shared. Recalling the origins of our gatherings as churches can help us see seemingly incidental actions, such as 'tea and biccies', in a much larger perspective. Looking at the past can show us what we do now, in very different ways, as reinterpretations, work-arounds, of basic aspects of discipleship. Then that leads on to the larger questions: should there be such a separation between the 'sacred' formally ritualized meal, 'the Eucharist' and the actual 'profane' informally ritualized meal? Is not every gathering of the Lord's people in the Lord's name a 'sacred event' in our actual world, just as he lived and ate in the midst of our actual world? And when we gather for even a token meal (coffee and biscuits in the church hall) should we not bless/thank the Father for his goodness for this assembly? And if we do that, then how is that gathering not as eucharistic as what took place in the church building?

Sustenance/boundary

When we look at the past we can see not only *what was done* but also *what was implicit in what was done*. In the early communities the boundary of the community was set by baptism (as is still formally the case for most Christians), and the Eucharist was what sustained the community and glued it together. For most Christians today, the Eucharist has become a boundary ritual: are you in communion with us, can you 'receive communion with us' or can I 'take/be given communion from you/by you'? In all such painful inter-Christian disputes there is no shortage of highly developed speculation. But if one has taken a wrong turning early in an argument, no matter how elaborate that argument becomes, it will still be heading in the wrong direction. One can create the most elaborate explanations of why there cannot be intercommunion between Christians, but fail to notice that the Eucharist was not intended as a boundary ritual but as a unifying and sustaining ritual. The assumption was that baptism forms the boundary, and then people's other differences are reconciled in the unity of Christ at his table. Here looking to the origins of what we do has the effect of undermining much later speculation as faulty. Here historical theology displays one of its most important functions: it allows us to 'check the wiring' of our arguments.

However, this sort of questioning based on examining the present in the light of the past is never easy! In the case of the simple comparison the task is to suggest 'improvements' in practice. For example, that there should be a 'real loaf' rather than token wafers or that 'we should all sit or stand around the table' at the Eucharist – this is the sort of thing that the Catholic Church has been attempting in its reforms of its practices since the 1960s – and there may be much to recommend this approach as a 'fix-it' strategy. But the more searching kind of comparison asks far more basic questions, is far more painful because most people are inordinately attached to their familiar rituals – though they will rarely admit it – but actually might touch the underlying fissures between Christians.

New Christians

The third example of historical comparison concerns how we envisage the task of making new Christians. This consists of the interlinked questions: first, why do we do it, and second, why do we do it in this way? The *Didache*'s primary purpose was the training of new members of a community, new believers in the Christ, and to guide new people on the Way. It was a task that was understood as pertaining to every existing member of the Church – though it is most unlikely that every Christian took an equal share in it. However, what is important is that the community was looking outwards and was adapting its approach, for instance, over the regulations of the law, to those it was encountering.

Looking at how and why they did this tells us a great deal about their sense of Christian identity, and it is by using these questions, inspired by examining the *Didache*, that we can ask the same questions of our communities today. For these questions will reveal our own sense of identity and purpose more quickly than any others. Here the *Didache* is not being held up as a model – though there are many excellent features in its approach – but as a screen which shows up to us our assumptions. It is worth remembering that the *Didache* was a success in what it set out to accomplish: it trained the early communities and they embedded the message of Christianity within their societies. The *Didache* was the means of effect-ively and simply transmitting their cherished way of life: a life based in divine wisdom and the notion of graced existence. Any group which cannot present itself as one wherein people are welcomed, a real community is established, and wisdom and grace, beauty and life are encountered, will not endure.

And finally . . .

This book has been an exploration of one short text from the first generations of Christians. I have tried to see through it to the communities that would have produced, valued and used a text like this as part of their everyday life as Christians. It was their text, and now, in a sense, it is our text also. Having worked through the *Didache* towards an appreciation of those churches, you may find that other books produced in those churches which we all too often simply think of as ours were first and foremost theirs. It is upon the tradition of those churches, as they sought to understand and witness to what the Father had done in the life, death and resurrection of Jesus, and how they sought to live as the community of the Anointed One, that the whole Christian edifice, in all its contemporary diversity, rests.

The Teaching of the Lord Given to the Gentiles by the Twelve Apostles

In most translations, there are notes inserted into the text or placed in footnotes pointing to sources or overlaps with other ancient texts. Such apparatus belongs to the world of reading, and would not have been heard when the Didache *was being used; rather the text would have 'rung bells' in the memories of the audience as they listened without being distracted as we tend to be by notes. So as to let the text simply ring bells in the memory, this translation is without notes.*

1.1 There are two ways: one is the Way of Life, the other is the Way of Death; and there is a mighty difference between these two ways.

1.2 The way of life is this: first, you shall love God who created you; second, your neighbour as yourself; all those things which you do not want to be done to you, you should not do to others.

1.3 The training about these words is this:
Bless those who curse you;
Pray for those who are your enemies;
Do fasts for those who persecute you.
What benefit is it if you love those who love you? Do not even the gentiles do that? Rather, you must love those who hate you, and so you are not to treat the other person as your enemy.

1.4 Abstain from carnal desires.
If someone strikes your left cheek, then turn the right cheek towards him also, and you will be perfect.
If someone makes you go one mile, then go the extra mile with him.

If someone takes your coat, then let him have your jacket.

If someone takes your property, then you are not allowed to ask for it back.

1.5 Give to everyone who asks help from you, and do not seek a return because the Father wants his generosity to be shared with everyone.

Blessed is anyone that gives according to this command, for that person goes without punishment. But, watch out for those who received these things: if they receive things from need, then there is no punishment, but if they receive these things without need then they shall have to explain why they acted in that way and they shall be questioned about it when in prison and they will not be released until the last penny is repaid.

1.6 But remember it has also been said that 'you should let your gift sweat in your hands until you know to whom to give it'.

2.1 Now, the second part of the training is this:

2.2 You shall not murder.

You shall not commit adultery.

You shall not corrupt boys.

You shall not be promiscuous.

You shall not steal.

You shall not practise divination.

You shall not practise with magic potions.

You shall not kill a child in the womb nor expose infants.

You shall not try to take your neighbours' goods.

2.3 You shall not perjure yourself.

You shall not act as a false witness.

You shall not speak evil of others.

You shall not hold grudges.

2.4 Do not be fickle or deceitful because the deceitful tongue is the snare of death.

2.5 Your discourse must neither be full of deceits nor empty, but rather it should be supported by your actions.

2.6 You should not be avaricious, nor greedy, nor hypocritical, nor spiteful, nor disdainful.

You should not be plotting against your neighbour.

2.7 You shall not hate anyone, rather you should correct some people, you should pray for other people, and yet others you should love more than your own life.

3.1 My child, run away from every kind of evil, and even from everything that looks like it.

3.2 Do not let yourself become angry: it may start in anger, but end in murder.
And do not be jealous, nor argumentative, nor someone with a hot temper: these can also end in murder.

3.3 My child, do not lust after sex, for such lust leads on to fornication.
You should not be someone of obscene speech nor someone with a roaming eye, for these too lead on to fornication.

3.4 My child, you must not become someone who works at telling the future by divination, for such doings lead on to idolatry. Nor should you be involved in casting magic spells, nor an astrologer, nor one who purges curses, nor should you allow yourself to become curious about these things, for they all lead on to idolatry.

3.5 My child, do not be one who tells lies, for lying leads on to thieving. And do not be greedy or vain, for these also lead on to thieving.

3.6 My child, do not be someone who grumbles, for it leads on to blasphemy. And do not be arrogant or bad-minded, for these too lead on to blasphemy.

3.7 Rather, you should act with humility for the humble shall inherit the earth.

3.8 You should be patient and merciful and without guile and quiet and good and you should treasure, with respect, these commandments you have received.

3.9 Do not be haughty, nor let your heart draw you off into false pride. You should not associate with the mighty, but live with the people who are righteous and humble.

3.10 Accept as blessings whatever happens to you, being aware that nothing happens without God.

4.1 My child, remember always, day and night, the one who speaks to you the discourse of God, and honour that person as you would the Lord: for wherever the things of the Lord are spoken about, there the Lord is present.

4.2 Furthermore, every day you should seek out the company of the saints so that you can be helped by their conversation.

4.3 Do not be someone who creates factions, rather work for reconciliation between parties. You should adjudicate with justice and so not show partiality when correcting transgressions.

4.4 You should not be someone who sits on the fence in these matters.

4.5 You should not be someone who opens his hands when it comes to receiving, but then keeps them shut when it comes to giving.

4.6 When you have earned your keep by the work of your hands, you should offer something for the expiation of your sins.

4.7 You must not be slow to be generous with alms, and do not grumble when you do give them, eventually you shall come to know who is the One who is the Good Paymaster who rewards all.

4.8 You must not turn away from anyone in need but share everything with your brother holding back nothing as just your individual property. Remember: if you are sharers in what is imperishable, how much more must you become sharers in what is perishable!

4.9 You should not keep back your hand from your son or daughter, but, from their youth, train them in the fear of the Lord.

4.10 You shall not give orders to your man-slave or woman-slave when you are angry – remember they hope in the same God as you – because this might cause them to stop respecting God who is over both of you; and remember that he comes to call, without thought of status, those whom the Spirit has prepared.

4.11 And slaves, you should be submissive to your masters with respect and fear as to an image of God.

4.12 You should hate all sham, and all that is not pleasing to the Lord.

4.13 You should not abandon the Lord's commands, but hold fast to what has been handed on to you without addition or subtraction.

4.14 You should acknowledge your transgressions in the church; and you should not set out on your prayers when you have a bad conscience.

This is the Way of Life.

5.1 Now, by contrast, here is the Way of Death.

First, it is full of wickedness and is cursed: it is full of murders, adulteries, lusts, acts of fornication, robberies, acts of idolatry, magic and sorcery, thefts, false accusations, sham, double dealing, fraud, arrogance, malicious intentions, stubbornness, covetousness, obscene language, jealousy, haughtiness, pride and pomposity.

5.2 This is the way of all those who persecute good people; of those who hate the truth and who love lies; of those who do not know the reward of righteousness, who are not devoted to what is good, and who do not give just judgements because they are not looking out for what is good but for what is evil. These people do not know gentleness, they lack patience, they love worthless things and pursue money. These people are without mercy for the poor, and do nothing on behalf of the oppressed.

These people do not know who was their Maker.

They are murderers of children, they are corrupters of God's image, they turn away from those in need, oppress the afflicted, are advocates of the wealthy, treat the poor unjustly.

All told, they are full of sin!

Children, may you be kept safe from all this.

6.1 Take care that no one leads you astray from this Way of the Teaching, because any other teaching takes you away from God.

6.2 Now if you are able to bear the whole of the Lord's yoke, you will be complete. However, if you are not able [to bear that yoke], then do what you can.

6.3 And concerning food regulations, bear what you are able. However, you must keep strictly away from meat that has been sacrificed to idols for involvement with it involves worship of dead gods.

7.1 With regard to baptism, here is the teaching:
You are to baptize in this way.
Once you have gone back over all that is in the Two Ways, you baptize in the name of the Father and of the Son and of the Holy Spirit in living water.

7.2 However, if you do not have access to living water, then baptize in some other water; and if you do not have any cold water, then you can use warm water.

7.3 And if you cannot get access to either [running or still water], then pour water three times on the head in the name of the Father and of the Son and of the Holy Spirit.

7.4 Moreover, before the baptism takes place, let both the person baptizing and the person who is going to be baptized fast – along with as many others as are able to do so. Indeed, you must instruct the person who is going to be baptized to fast for one or two days before the baptism.

8.1 You must not let your days of fasting be at the same time as those of the hypocrites. They fast on the second day of the sabbath and on the fifth day of the sabbath, so you should hold your fasts on the fourth day of the sabbath and on the Day of Preparation.

8.2 Nor should you offer prayers as the hypocrites do.
Rather, you should pray like this, just as the Lord commanded in his gospel:

Our Father, who is in the heaven
Hallowed be your name
Your kingdom come
Your will be done on earth as it is in heaven
Give us this day our daily bread
And forgive us our debt as we forgive our debtors
And do not lead us in the trial
But deliver us from evil
For yours is the power and glory for ever.

8.3 Say this prayer three times each day.

9.1 Now this is how you should engage in giving thanks, bless God in this way.

9.2 First, at the cup, say:

> We give thanks to you, our Father,
> for the holy vine of David, your servant, which you have
> made known to us.
> Through Jesus, your servant, to you be glory for ever.

9.3 Then when it comes to the broken loaf say:

> We give thanks to you, our Father,
> for the life and knowledge which you have made known
> to us.
> Through Jesus, your servant, to you be glory for ever.

9.4 For as the broken loaf was once scattered over the mountains and then was gathered in and became one, so may your church be gathered together into your kingdom from the very ends of the earth.

> Yours is the glory and the power through Jesus Christ for ever.

9.5 Only let those who have been baptized in the name of the Lord eat and drink at your Eucharists. And remember what the Lord has said about this: do not give to dogs what is holy.

10.1 After you all have had enough to eat, give thanks in this way:

10.2 We give you thanks, holy Father, for your holy name which you have made to dwell in our hearts, and for the knowledge and faith and immortality which you have made known to us.

> Through Jesus, your servant, to you be glory for ever.

10.3 You are the mighty ruler of all who has created all for your name's sake, and you have given food and drink to human beings for their enjoyment so that they might give thanks to you. But to us, from your generosity, you have given spiritual food and drink, and life eternal, through your servant.

10.4 Above all things we give thanks to you because you are mighty: to you be glory for ever.

10.5 Remember, Lord, your church, deliver her from evil, make her complete in your love, and gather her from the four winds into your kingdom you have prepared for her, for yours is the power and the glory for ever.

10.6   May grace come and may this world pass away.

Hosanna to the God of David.

If anyone is holy, let him advance; if anyone is not, let him be converted.

Maranatha. Amen.

10.7   However, permit the prophets to give thanks in whatever manner they wish.

11.1   Now, whoever comes to you and teaches all these things which have just been set out here, you are to welcome him.

11.2   However, if a teacher has himself wandered from the right path and has begun to teach a teaching that is at odds with what is set out here, you should not listen to him.

On the other hand, if his teaching promotes holiness and knowledge of the Lord, then you should welcome him as you would the Lord.

11.3   Now, turning to apostles and prophets you must treat them according to the rule of the gospel.

11.4   Every apostle who arrives among you is to be welcomed as if he were the Lord.

11.5   But normally he must not stay with you for more than one day, but he may stay a second day if this is necessary. However, if he stays a third day, then he is a false prophet!

11.6   When he leaves you, an apostle must receive nothing except enough food to sustain him until the next night's lodgings. However, if he asks for money, then he is a false prophet!

11.7   Now if any prophet speaks in the Spirit he is not to be tested: for every sin can be forgiven but this sin cannot be forgiven.

11.8   However, not everyone who speaks in the Spirit is a prophet: only those who show that they follow the Way of the Lord. It is by the way that he lives that the true prophet can be separated from the false one.

11.9   Now if a prophet speaking in the Spirit orders a banquet, then that man should not partake in it; if he does eat the meal, then he is a false prophet.

11.10 And any prophet who teaches the truth, but does not live according to his teaching is to be considered a false prophet.

11.11 Any prophet, who has been proven to be a true prophet, who acts out in his life the earthly mystery of the church (provided that he does not teach everyone to do as he does) is not to be judged by you: leave his judgement with God. After all, the prophets in olden times also acted in that way.

11.12 Now if anyone should say in the Spirit 'Give me money' – or anything like that – you should not listen to that man; however, if he tells you to give something to other people who are in need, then he is not to be condemned.

12.1 Now anyone coming in the Lord's name should be made welcome; then you can test him, using your own insight [into human nature] to see if he is genuine or a fraud.

12.2 If the visitor is someone who is passing through, help him as much as you can. However, he is not to stay for more than two days – or three out of necessity.

12.3 If the visitor wishes to settle in your community, then, if he is a craftsman, he should work for his living.

12.4 But if he does not have a trade, then use your own judgement to decide how he is to live among you as a Christian: but he is not to live in idleness.

12.5 If he is unhappy with this arrangement, then he is a 'christmonger'. Be on the watch for such people.

13.1 Any true prophet who wishes to settle down among you is worthy of his food. In the same way, any true teacher is like a labourer who is worthy of his food.

13.2 So take the first fruits of the vine and the harvest, of cattle and sheep, and present these first fruits to the prophets because they are, to you, the high priests.

13.3 But if you have no prophet [settled in your community], then give the first fruits to the poor.

13.4 When you bake a batch of bread, take the first loaf and present it as it says in the commandment.

13.5 Do likewise when you open a fresh flask of wine or oil: take the first portion from it and present it to the prophets.

13.6 So also with money and cloth and other commodities: set aside the first fruits, and give it – as much as seems right to you – according to the commandment.

14.1 On the day which is the Day of the Lord gather together for the breaking of the loaf and giving thanks. However, you should first confess your sins so that your sacrifice may be a pure one;

14.2 and do not let anyone who is having a dispute with a neighbour join until they are reconciled so that your sacrifice may not be impure.

14.3 For this is the sacrifice about which the Lord has said: 'In every place and time let a pure sacrifice be offered to me, for I am the great king, says the Lord, and my name is feared among the nations.'

15.1 Select for yourselves bishops and deacons: men who are worthy of the Lord, humble, not greedy for money, honest, and well tested, because these too carry out for you the service of the prophets and teachers.

15.2 Therefore, you should not despise them but treat them as your honoured men like the prophets and teachers.
Now when you come to correct one another, this is to be done in a composed way, and not in anger, just as you find in the gospel.

15.3 And when someone does wrong against his neighbour, let no one speak to him, indeed he is not to hear anything from you, until he repents.

15.4 Now with regard to your prayers and almsgiving, indeed all your actions, do them all in the way that you find them prescribed in our Lord's gospel.

16.1 Watch over your lives. You must not let your lamps go out, nor should you let your loins be ungirded, rather you should be ready because you do not know the hour at which our Lord is coming.

16.2 Gather together frequently and seek those things that are good for your souls. Otherwise what use will having faith over all the time of your life be to you, if at the end of time you are not made perfect.

16.3 For in the last days there are going to be many false prophets and those who would corrupt you, then the sheep will turn into wolves, and love will turn into hate.

16.4 Then when lawlessness is increasing, people will hate and persecute and be treacherous with one another. Then, indeed, the Deceiver of this world will appear as if a son of God and he will do signs and wonders and the earth will be delivered into his hands and he will commit lawless acts such as have never been seen since the world began.

16.5 Then all people will be brought through the trial of fire. Then many will fall away and will perish; but those who stand firm in their faith will be saved by the Cursed One himself.

16.6 And then, the signs of the truth will appear:
The first sign will be the heavens opening;
Then [second,] the sound of the trumpet;
And, third, the resurrection of the dead –

16.7 but not of everyone, but as it has been said: 'the Lord will come and all his saints with him.'

16.8 Then the world will see the Lord coming upon the clouds of heaven.

Further reading

Facsimile of the manuscript

Harris, J. Rendel (1887), *The Teaching of the Apostles (Didache tōn Apostolōn): Newly Edited, with Facsimile Text and a Commentary*, London: Clay & Sons.

Editions of the *Didache* in Greek

The Apostolic Fathers, vol. 1, ed. and trans. Bart D. Ehrman, *Loeb Classical Library* 24, Cambridge, Mass.; London, Harvard University Press, 2003, 403–43.

Holmes, Michael William, ed. (1992), *The Apostolic Fathers: Greek Texts and English Translations of Their Writings*, trans. and ed. J. B. Lightfoot and J. R. Harmer, 2nd edn, Grand Rapids, Mich., Baker Book House, 246–69.

Milavec, Aaron (2004), *The Didache: Text, Translation, Analysis, and Commentary*, Collegeville, Minn., Liturgical Press.

Commentaries

There are two full-length, recent commentaries on the *Didache*:

Milavec, Aaron (2003), *The Didache: Faith, Hope, and Life of the Earliest Christian Communities, 50–70 C.E.*, New York, Newman Press.

Niederwimmer, Kurt (1998), *The Didache: A Commentary*, trans. Linda M. Maloney, ed. Harold W. Attridge, Minneapolis, Fortress Press.

Works referred to in this book

Achtemeier, P. J. (1990), '*Omne verbum sonat*: The New Testament and the Oral Environment of Late Western Antiquity', *Journal of Biblical Literature* 109, 3–27.

Aharoni, Y., et al. (2003), *Historical Atlas of the Jewish People*, New York; London, Continuum.

Aldridge, R. E. (1999), 'The Lost Ending of the *Didache*', *Vigiliae Christianae* 53, 1–15.

Audet, J.-P. (1959), 'Literary Forms and Contents of a Normal *Eucharistia* in the First Century', in K. Aland, F. L. Cross, J. Daniélou, H. Riesenfeld and W. C. van Unnik, eds, *Studia Evangelica* I, Berlin, 643–62.

Audet, J.-P. (1996), 'Literary and Doctrinal Relationships of the "Manual of Discipline"', in Jonathan A. Draper, ed., *The Didache in Modern Research*, Leiden, Brill [originally in French, 1952], 129–47.

Bauckham, R., ed. (1998), *The Gospels for All Christians: Rethinking the Gospel Audience*, Edinburgh, T & T Clark.

Bloch, Marc (1992), *The Historian's Craft*, Manchester, Manchester University Press [originally in French, 1944].

Bradshaw, P. (1979), 'Prayer Morning, Noon, Evening, and Midnight – an Apostolic Custom?', *Studia Liturgica* 13, 57–62.

Charlesworth, J. H. (1983), *The Old Testament Pseudepigrapha, Vol. I: Apocalyptic Literature and Testaments*, London, Doubleday.

Cohn, Norman (1970), *The Pursuit of the Millennium: Revolutionary Millenarians and Mystical Anarchists of the Middle Ages*, rev. edn, New York, Oxford University Press.

Collins, J. J. (1984), *The Apocalyptic Imagination: An Introduction to the Jewish Matrix of Christianity*, New York, Crossroad.

Daly-Denton, M. (2008), 'Looking beyond the Upper Room: Eucharistic Origins in Contemporary Research', *Search* 31, 3–15.

Draper, J. A. (2006a), 'The Apostolic Fathers: The Didache', *Expository Times* 117, 177–81.

Draper, J. A. (2006b), 'First-fruits and the Support of the Prophets, Teachers, and the Poor in *Didache* 13 in Relation to New Testament Parallels', in Andrew F. Gregory and Christopher M. Tuckett, eds, *Trajectories through the New Testament and the Apostolic Fathers*, Oxford, Oxford University Press, 223–43.

Finkelstein, L. (1929), 'The Birkat ha-Mazon', *Jewish Quarterly Review* 19, 211–62.

Foster, P. (2006), 'The Epistles of Ignatius of Antioch', *Expository Times* 117, 487–95, and 118, 2–11 [article in two parts].

Frend, W. H. C. (2003), *From Dogma to History: How Our Understanding of the Early Church Developed*, London, SCM Press.

García Martínez, Florentino (1994), *The Dead Sea Scrolls Translated: The Qumran Texts in English*, trans. Wilfred G. E. Watson, Leiden, Brill.

Garrow, Alan John Philip (2004), *The Gospel of Matthew's Dependence on the Didache*, Journal for the Study of the New Testament Supplement Series 254, London, T & T Clark International.

Gregory, A. (2006), '*I Clement*: An Introduction', *Expository Times* 117, 223–30.

Henderson, I. H. (1992), '*Didache* and Orality in Synoptic Comparison', *Journal of Biblical Literature* 111, 283–306.

Jewett, R. (1994), 'Gospel and Commensality: Social and Theological Implications of Galatians 2.14', in L. A. Jervis and P. Richardson, eds, *Gospel in Paul: Studies on Corinthians, Galatians and Romans for Richard N. Longenecker*, Journal for the Study of the New Testament Supplement Series 108, Sheffield, Sheffield Academic Press, 240–52.

Ligier, L. (1973), 'The Origins of the Eucharistic Prayer', *Studia Liturgica* 9, 161–85.

McGowan, Andrew Brian (1999), *Ascetic Eucharists: Food and Drink in Early Christian Ritual Meals*, Oxford, Clarendon Press.

McKendrick, S. (2006), *In a Monastery Library: Preserving Codex Sinaiticus and the Greek Written Heritage*, London, British Library.

Maher, M. (2003), 'Knowing the Tree by Its Roots: Jewish Context of the Early Christian Movement', in K. O'Mahony, ed., *Christian Origins: Worship, Belief and Society*, Journal for the Study of the New Testament Supplement Series 241, Sheffield, Sheffield Academic Press, 1–28.

Meeks, Wayne A. (2003), *The First Urban Christians: The Social World of the Apostle Paul*, 2nd edn, New Haven, Conn.; London, Yale University Press.

Meier, John P. (1994), *A Marginal Jew: Rethinking the Historical Jesus vol. 2: Mentor, Message, and Miracles*, New York; London, Doubleday.

Meier, John P. (2001), *A Marginal Jew: Rethinking the Historical Jesus vol. 3: Companions and Competitors*, New York; London, Doubleday.

Milavec, A. (1989), 'The Pastoral Genius of the *Didache*: An Analytical Translation and Commentary', in J. Neusner, E. S. Frerichs and A. J. Levine, eds, *Religious Writings and Religious Systems II: Christianity*, Atlanta, Ga., Scholars Press, 89–126.

Milavec, A. (1994), 'Distinguishing True and False Prophets: The Protective Wisdom of the *Didache*', *Journal of Early Christian Studies* 2, 117–36.

Moore, Carey A. (1985), *Judith: A New Translation with Introduction and Commentary*, Anchor Bible 40, New York, Doubleday.

Murphy-O'Connor, Jerome (1976), 'Eucharist and Community in First Corinthians' [part 1], *Worship* 50, 370–85.

Murphy-O'Connor, Jerome (1977), 'Eucharist and Community in First Corinthians' [part 2], *Worship* 51, 56–69.

Murphy-O'Connor, Jerome (1996), *Paul: A Critical Life*, Oxford, Clarendon Press.

Newman, John Henry (1890), 'Reformation of the XIth Century', *Essays Critical and Historical*, vol. 2, 10th edn, London, Longmans Green.

Nodet, Étienne, and Taylor, Justin (1998), *The Origins of Christianity: An Exploration*, Collegeville, Minn., Liturgical Press.

O'Loughlin, T. (2000), 'Penitentials and Pastoral Care', in G. R. Evans, ed., *A History of Pastoral Care*, London, Cassell, 93–111.

O'Loughlin, T. (2003a), 'The Didache as a Source for Picturing the Earliest Christian Communities: The Case of the Practice of Fasting', in K. O'Mahony, ed., *Christian Origins: Worship, Belief and Society*, Journal for the Study of the New Testament Supplement Series 241, Sheffield, Sheffield Academic Press, 83–112.

O'Loughlin, T. (2003b) 'The Praxis and Explanations of Eucharistic Fraction in the Ninth Century: The Insular Evidence', *Archiv für Liturgiewissenschaft* 45, 1–20.

O'Loughlin, T. (2004), 'Translating *Panis* in a Eucharistic Context: A Problem of Language and Theology', *Worship* 78, 226–35.

O'Loughlin, T. (2009), 'Another Post-Resurrection Meal and Its Implications for the Early Understanding of the Eucharist', in Zuleika Rodgers with Margaret Daly-Denton and Anne Fitzpatrick McKinley, eds, *A Wandering Galilean: Essays in Honour of Seán Freyne*, Leiden, Brill, 485–503.

Parvis, P. (2006), '2 Clement and the Meaning of the Christian Homily', *Expository Times* 117, 265–70.

Riddle, D. W. (1938), 'Early Christian Hospitality: A Factor in the Gospel Transmission', *Journal of Biblical Literature* 57, 141–54.

Rordorf, W. (1980–2), 'The Lord's Prayer in the Light of Its Liturgical Use in the Early Church', *Studia Liturgica* 14, 1–19.

Rothenbuhler, Eric W. (1998), *Ritual Communication: From Everyday Conversation to Mediated Ceremony*, Thousand Oaks, Calif.; London, Sage Publications.

Rowland, Christopher (1982), *The Open Heaven: A Study of Apocalyptic in Judaism and Early Christianity*, London, SPCK.

Schaff, Philip (1885), *The Oldest Church Manual called The Teaching of the Twelve Apostles*, New York, Funk & Wagnalls.

Smith, Dennis Edwin (1987), 'Table Fellowship as a Literary Motif in the Gospel of Luke', *Journal of Biblical Literature* 106, 613–38.

Smith, Dennis Edwin (2003), *From Symposium to Eucharist: The Banquet in the Early Christian World*, Minneapolis, Fortress Press.

Smith, Jonathan Z. (1990), *Drudgery Divine: On the Comparison of Early Christianities and the Religions of Late Antiquity*, London, School of Oriental and African Studies, University of London.

Stanton, Graham (2004), *Jesus and Gospel*, Cambridge, Cambridge University Press.

Stewart-Sykes, A. (2004), 'The Birkath ha-Mazon and the Body of the Lord: A Case-study of Didache 9–10', *Questions Liturgiques* 85, 197–205.

Sullivan, Francis Aloysius (2001), *From Apostles to Bishops: The Development of the Episcopacy in the Early Church*, New York, Paulist Press.

Taft, R. (2003), 'Mass without the Consecration?', *America* (12 May).

Talley, Thomas J. (1986), *The Origins of the Liturgical Year*, New York, Pueblo Pub. Co.

Taussig, Hal (2009), *In the Beginning was the Meal: Social Experimentation and Early Christian Identity*, Minneapolis, Fortress Press.

Theissen, G. (1982), *The Social Setting of Pauline Christianity*, Edinburgh, T & T Clark.

Thompson, E. P. (1967), 'Time, Work-Discipline, and Industrial Capitalism', *Past & Present* 38, 56–97.

Thompson, M. B. (1998), 'The Holy Internet: Communication between Churches in the First Christian Generation', in Bauckham (1998), 49–70.

Varner, W. C. (2008), 'The *Didache* "Apocalypse" and Matthew 24', *Bibliotheca Sacra* 165, 309–22.

Verheyden, J. (2005), 'Eschatology in the Didache and the Gospel of Matthew', in H. van de Sandt, ed., *Matthew and the Didache: Two Documents from the Same Jewish-Christian Milieu?*, Assen, Royal Van Gorcum; Minneapolis, Fortress Press, 193–215.

Vermes, Geza (1962), *The Dead Sea Scrolls in English*, Harmondsworth, Penguin.

Yarbro Collins, Adela (1984), *Crisis and Catharsis: The Power of the Apocalypse*, Philadelphia, Pa., Westminster Press.

Index of biblical and ancient texts

Index of authors and subjects